Play Stronger Chess By Examining Chess960

Usable Strategies of
Fischer Random Chess
Discovered

Gene Milener

Castle Long Publications

Publisher's Cataloging-in-Publication Data
Milener, Eugene Darden.
    Play stronger chess by examining chess960 : usable strategies of Fischer random chess discovered / Gene Milener.
    p. cm.
    ISBN 0-9774521-0-7
1. Chess. 2. Chess--Rules. 3. Chess--Openings 4. Chess--Collections of games
5. Chess--Psychological aspects. I. Title.
GV1446.M55 2006
794.122--dc22

Castle Long Publications
Renton, WA   98058
USA

First edition. First copy printed in January 2006.

Logo for CLP: A Handy Symmato 3D rook icon.

For information and inquiries see our web site:
http://www.CastleLong.com/

Acknowledgments

This book could not exist without the successes of Hans-Walter Schmitt and the Chess Tigers organization he represents. The Chess Tigers have attracted the world's elite chess players to their annual chess960 tournaments. Gratitude is due to the FiNet AG company, and to the Livingson company, for their direct financial support of the fledgling chess960. It is my hope that this book will further the cause of chess960 for which the Chess Tigers have so labored during the past several years.

I am blessed with a family that agreeably afforded me the time needed to accomplish this work. Credit is due to my wife Amy Eaton and to our daughters Patia and Sara, for their help with proofreading and my back cover photograph. To them all I say thank you for indulging me in so many discussions about chess.

Contents

Handy Symmato 3D king.

About the Author

My surname is pronounced MILL-enn-urr. I was born in Brooklyn and was raised in Oneonta, NY, USA. I spent my childhood playing tennis and Strat-O-Matic sports games. I studied Human Experimental Psychology in graduate school, where I met Amy. I feed my family as a software developer. I was an original member of the team that created the Microsoft .NET Common Language Runtime, a project that began hushed in 1997 and released in 2002.

After crashing one too many radio controlled racing cars several years ago, I aroused my hibernating interest in chess. I enjoy exchanging ideas about chess as a player, a reader, and a writer. I encourage chess players to attend their local chess club. There you can shake hands with your opponent and talk to his face. Play in some games that matter, play in USCF rated tournaments. Come win some, come lose some. The chess club is what sociologist Ray Oldenburg would call a great third place.

Introduction

What is Chess960?:   This is a chess book, one that uses chess960 as a tool to better understand chess.   My informal observations tell me that most active tournament chess players know what Fischer Random Chess is, though some are hazy on the details.   Many are unaware that the name chess960 is replacing the old tentative names of Fischer Random Chess or Fischerandom or FRC.

Most chess players in America never join the USCF (United States Chess Federation) and they never play in rated tournaments.   A large percentage of these casual chess players are barely aware of chess960 or FRC.   I must address this briefly before I can proceed.   Later in the book much more detail will be given.

In traditional chess, or what this book calls chess1, the same initial setup of White and Black pieces is used over and over for every game.   In chess960 White's pieces on row 1 are randomly placed only minutes before the game starts, as determined by dice.   On row 8, each Black piece is setup on the same column as the matching White piece.   One possible setup is the chess1 setup.   This random selection of the setup is the only rule change from chess1.

Each valid setup must obey two restrictions.   First, the two bishops must start on opposite shade squares.   Second, the king must be between the two rooks. Once the moves begin, chess960 is just chess.

One goal of chess960 is to reduce the effects of memorized and repetitious opening moves. The other goal is to gain access to a vast untapped cache of new and interesting patterns and tactical strategies in chess play.

Chess Book Formats: In the world of chess books there are two dominant formats, neither of which is used for this book. One format is to have many chapters each devoted to a few annotated chess games. The other format focuses on a given well known traditional chess opening, such as the Ruy Lopez or the Sicilian Defense.

This chess book does look deeply into the opening phase of chess, but not in any way you have seen before in any other book. This book approaches 250 pages in length, yet you could count on your fingers the full chess960 games it contains. The full games this book does contain are annotated, almost at every ply, but not in any way you have seen before. Whatever its strengths and weaknesses, this book does not cover the same chess topics that have already been covered multiple times by the other chess books on your shelf. The territory and ideas covered in this book are so new and novel that I found myself wishing someone else had already written something in depth about chess960, something I could use to guide my own efforts. Instead I had no previous work on which to build.

Chess960 is Just Chess: This book is about chess960. Chess960 is so similar to traditional chess1 that any book about chess960 is automatically also about chess in general. Many chess books exclaim that paying customers will learn valuable "secrets" about chess, or that "explosive" opening techniques will be learned. The implication is that increased Elo ratings will come to players who read them. These overly optimistic claims are forgiven in much the same way we forgive artistic license in an enjoyable movie. It never hurts to have an additional exposure to a useful opening or middle game idea, but often the explosive secrets are already covered in books written long ago. I promise the chess players who buy this book that they will be exposed to chess ideas that truly are new.

Two Other Chess960 Books: To my knowledge as of December 2005 there have been only two other books written on the topic of chess960. The first was *Shall We Play Fischerandom Chess?* written in 2002 by former WCC (World Chess Champion) candidate Svetozar Gligoric. I was quite curious when I first opened Gligoric's book. I found in it discussions that surrounded the central topic without ever addressing chess960 playing strategies directly. Gligoric claimed only to discuss the history of ideas similar to chess960, and to collect contemporary opinions about chess960, and opinions about the current problems with traditional chess, and to show a few annotated chess960 games. Gligoric delivered well on those claims. But I was hoping for some penetrating intellectual analysis of chess960 itself.

The other chess960 book is *Fischer-Random-Chess (FRC/Chess960): The Revolutionary Future of Chess (Including Computer Chess)*, which was authored by Reinhard Scharnagl in 2004. The book is published only in German. I have translated his table of contents, so I believe I understand the range he sought to cover. Scharnagl's book covers some important topics that Gligoric did not. One such topic is his ideas for handling FEN and PGN computer notations for chess games, in a manner that also meets the needs of chess960. His book also introduced the chess960 three digit setup Id system that is most widely used today. Scharnagl's book does not attempt to penetrate into the strategies and tactics of chess960 itself.

There is a Lot to Say: I began writing this book before I realized that was what I was doing. I thought I was just taking notes on ideas and realizations that came to me as I became interested in understanding chess960 at a more analytical level. As my first notebook became full and gave way to my second, it slowly dawned on me that there was a lot that needed to be studied and reported about chess960 itself. This was almost a paradox because it had also become clear to me that chess960 is just chess, it is not a "variant" of traditional chess1. Pure chess is incomplete without chess960. I realized that by comparing and relating chess960 and chess1 we can all achieve a deeper understanding of both of these chess rule sets.

Bobby Fischer had sound but negative reasons for inventing his refinement of the older shuffle chess ideas: he was looking to fix problems in chess1. While I still see merit in Fischer's arguments, I came to realize they are secondary to the positive reasons why the chess world at large should want to give chess960 a chance. Fischer feels "old chess" has nothing left to contribute to chess in general. I disagree, and I explain why in this book. I like both chess960 and chess1, and both add their own kinds of desirable aspects to fundamental chess that the other cannot.

Many Ways to Enjoy Chess: For chess enthusiasts there are many ways to enjoy chess beyond playing. Many players enjoy the formality and discipline of tournament competition. Many enjoy studying games played by others. Some like to teach chess to youngsters. Some like to research the history of chess. Some like to compose endgame puzzles. Some like to collect interesting chess sets. Some design cool chess fonts or pieces. Some like to write chess books, about which others like to write reviews. A precious few run tournaments or chess clubs. The list goes on. This book is for the enjoyment of chess enthusiasts who want to think about and converse on a wide range of issues in chess, just for the intellectual stimulation of new ideas. This book is also for players who want to understand chess1 and pure fundamental chess at a deeper level. Of course, this book is also for players who want to begin an analytical understanding of chess960 strategies and tactics.

Who should try chess960?: WCC Vasily Smyslov wrote that to be great at chess a player first has to "learn what the pieces can do". A new chess960 player learns the pieces are called upon to coordinate in patterns unfamiliar from chess1. If you want to gain a deeper command of the pieces used in traditional chess1, study and play some chess960. If you are a player who does not remember traditional opening trees both broadly and deeply, then you should play some chess960. If raw memorization has not worked for your opening play and you would like to learn about alternative approaches to understanding the opening phase, you should read this book and play some chess960 games. If you assume the basic opening principles Aron Nimzovich described in his book *My System* are pure and true regardless of the initial setup behind the pawns, you should read this book and play some chess960 games. If you believe rooks are inherently pieces that cannot contribute until the early middle game, you should read this book. If you would like to feel more comfortable and confident in your traditional chess games that go out of book early, then you should play some chess960 games. It is true that chess960 games feel just like traditional chess games before the opening is completed. This has led to a casual consensus opinion that the chess960 middle games offer nothing beyond what chess1 offers. If you would like to know why this consensus must be revised, you should read this book. If you feel there is more to be enjoyed about chess than just the latest published opening book or the latest published grandmaster game, then you should read this book. And play some chess960.

Formal Recognition: I have one final point to make here in this introduction. The USCF should formally recognize and sanction chess960. This should be in the form of announcing that chess960 results can be submitted for formal rating just like any chess1 results.

Gene Milener
December 2005

Part 1

Beyond the Board

"The questions you ask set limits on the answers you find."
    - *Temple Grandin, from* Animals in Translation

An informal statement of the rules for chess960 (or FRC) can be quite brief. The two bishops must start on different shade squares, and the king must start between the two rooks. After castling, the king and rook end on the same squares they always have. Done.

Chess960 is a drastic change in the initial setup. But in chess everything is at least transitively connected to everything else. Changing the setup affects many other things, not just the moves played during the opening phase. Terminology is affected. Notation is affected. Philosophical issues about chess are raised. How much weight should be given to tradition for its own sake? What exactly is a 'variant' of chess? Should chess960 advocates prefer to replace traditional chess1 or to attain full equality with it? Would there be a looming problem of a WCC title split, one for chess1 and another for chess960?

What kind of recognition should be made of chess960 by the USCF? Is chess960 just a solution to the traditional problem of repetitious opening moves, or is chess960 our opportunity to discover and harvest portions of the larger chess realm that have long been hidden from us? Are there other problems beyond the openings in chess1 that chess960 might be able to address? Part 1 will address topics like these. Discussions about the strategic and tactical ideas particular to chess960 will be discussed in Part 2.

Bobby Fischer announced his invention of FRC in 1996. I am not aware of any serious efforts he has since made to promote it. Others have stepped up to provide leadership and accomplishment in the promotion and growth of chess960, and we will be looking at the great work they have been doing. We will look at fine tuning the current rules of chess960. We will also examine ideas for additional rule changes for chess960.

1
Terminology
and
CRAN Notation

Chess960 is new. Not surprisingly it brings with it the need for some new terminology. Chess960 also gives us reason to revisit and refine some existing terminology. In this next section I define or refine terms that are needed before we can delve into our serious discussions.

Terms Needed Immediately

chess: In this book 'chess' is the *general* term for the fundamental game we all love, without being specific to either chess1 or chess960. Chess was invented in roughly the period from 1400-1475 AD. Chess implies a partial rule set, like an 8x8 board of checkered squares, alternating turns, checkmate of the king, the types of pieces and their basic powers of movement and capture, and pawn promotion. Chess variants, like Bughouse chess or Progressive chess or Fairy chess or Janus chess or Superchess, are not included in this term because they deviate too greatly from this fundamental description for chess. Of course, this general term 'chess' has been used traditionally to mean 'chess1', a legacy practice with inherent bias that should be avoided when chess960 is part of the discussion.

chess1: 'Chess1' is chess with the particular rule set used almost exclusively since around the year 1475 AD. Non-trivial variations within this rule set occurred over the years, such as whether a stalemate was a win or a draw, the details about castling, and the details surrounding pawn promotion. But for our purposes its major feature is its total restriction of the initial setup of the pieces behind the pawns to the same one arrangement used for every game. That single setup has been extensively researched and pre-calculated, with the findings published in massive databases of opening trees. Chess1 has not been exhausted, but its opening phase has long since fallen into frequent repetition. As will be explained further, we name the chess1 setup R#362 or S#518, and from column 'a' to 'h' this setup can be represented as RNBQ-KBNR.

chess960: 'Chess960' is a particular implementation of the general concept of chess. Chess960 is a rule set. The chess960 rule set is nearly identical to the rules of FRC. The difference between FRC and chess960 is that the details within the chess960 rule set are eligible for improvements if some are found. The only difference between chess1 and chess960 is that in chess960 neither player knows which of the valid 960 setups will be randomly chosen until minutes before the game starts.

Fischer Random Chess: 'Fischer Random Chess' is a fading term for chess960. This is best abbreviated as FRC. This name captures the chess rule set as it was announced by its inventor Bobby Fischer on June 19, 1996. By definition, the particulars of this rule set cannot be adjusted or improved. The consensus among the world's grandmasters that participate in serious FRC play was that the name had to be changed, and they settled on chess960. Chess960 begins with the exact same rule set as FRC, but at this very early stage some particulars of the chess960 rule set are eligible for adjustment or improvements as tournament directors and consensus see fit.

mirror: The concept of symmetry on the *same* wing. For instance, in the opening plair 1. b24 b75 each ply could be considered the mirror of the other, being symmetrical on the 'a' wing. Compare with reciprocal.

plair: One White ply followed by one Black ply. The noun 'move' is ambiguous. Sometimes it means one ply, other times two. This term plair is better than attempts like 'move-pair' or 'ply-pair'.

ply: One move by one player. Compare with plair.

R#362: This is the numeric identifier for the traditional setup of the pieces on rank 1 in columns a-h, RNBQ-KBNR. Another numeric system calls this setup S#518.

reciprocal: The concept of symmetry on the *opposite* wing. For instance, in the opening plair 1. a23 h76 each ply could be considered the reciprocal of the other. The possible chess960 initial setup RNBK-QBNR is the reciprocal of the traditional chess1 setup. Compare with mirror.

Abbreviations and Acronyms

FIDE: Federation International of Chess (fee-DAA)
FRC: Fischer Random Chess
USCF: United State Chess Federation
WCC: World Chess Champion

Concise Reversible Algebraic Notation (CRAN)

Reading and following chess move notation for a chess960 game can be slightly more error prone than for chess1, because the pieces stand on a greater variety of squares. Partly to eliminate this problem, a reversible form of algebraic notation is used in this chess book. I call it CRAN. See if you already understand CRAN: what movements on the board are represented by 1. d24 Ne8f6? If you answered 1. d2-d4 Ne8-f6, you understand CRAN.

Reversible: In the world of chess publishing there is a surprisingly wide variety of algebraic notations used, including semi-reversible notations. Despite all the variety, I know of no other modern book or publication that predominantly uses a fully reversible form of chess notation, algebraic or otherwise. Perhaps the absurdly verbose notation formats used hundreds of years ago by Andre Danican Philidor and Howard Staunton were fully reversible. For a notation to earn the attribute of reversible, it must be possible to replay the game in reverse given the ending position or a mid-game diagram. Each ply should be replay-able in reverse without any need to examine other plies.

In the small table below, one ply is notated a variety of ways. Which notations are the most informative and are the only reversible notations?

Rd6	MAN (Minimal Algebraic Notation)
Rxd6	SAN (Standard Algebraic Notation)
Rd2xd6	LAN (Long Algebraic Notation)
Rd2xBd6	RAN (Reversible Algebraic Notation)
Rd2:B6	CRAN (Concise Reversible Algebraic Notation)

The last two notations are the only ones sufficiently informative to be reversible. The only information lacking is the color of the rook and taken bishop.

To understand any RAN, just remember that the first two coordinates will *always* be a letter-number pair dedicated to the origin square of the piece being moved. The destination square coordinates follow.

Concise: This book uses a Concise RAN, abbreviated CRAN. In CRAN any part of the destination square coordinates that is redundant with the origin square coordinates is omitted. CRAN discards the dash or minus sign ('-') used in LAN, because the eye does not need it. The dash is used in notation only rarely, as a placeholder for absent information, like Q-g3 when the origin square is unknown. Thus CRAN notates P-K4 as e65, not as e6-e5. Where LAN says Rd6-g6 CRAN instead says Rd6g. In CRAN the dash or minus sign is generally reserved for more important annotation usage (to indicate Black has a better position).

I have never liked the choice of a lower case letter 'x' for denoting "takes". Algebraic notation already has oodles of letters in it including eight lower case letters. Why unnecessarily add the distraction of a ninth lower case letter? Some chess publications, like Informant, save precious space by omitting the technically unnecessary takes symbol, knowing many chess players find the omission irritating to the eye. A few publications use the colon symbol ':' for takes, and CRAN adopts that. However, I would like to encourage the chess world to use ':' for takes only when information about the type of piece taken will always be provided (though usually the P for pawn should be omitted). Otherwise use 'x' or nothing.

Errors: Everyone who interacts with chess notation makes errors, both in reading and in writing notation. In practice, usage of CRAN notation eliminates entire classes of errors commonly seen where SAN is used. CRAN eliminates a class of inter-language errors. If an American reading a German chess publication finds ambiguity when struggling to interpret the notation De4, CRAN can eliminate that ambiguity with Df4e, because the leading 'D' becomes non-essential. Common replay errors from books or personal score sheets are greatly reduced. People impulsively think of the notation e4 as being the move of a White pawn, when of course if could just as easily mean e54. Such human tendencies are only one source of replay errors, a source CRAN eliminates.

Errors occur when trying to reset the pieces after pursuing a middle game variation. CRAN's extras ease this problem. With CRAN, readers more often can follow a variation without needing to disturb the pieces. For this same underlying reason, CRAN is better for students reading chess puzzle books, who must flip back and forth between the diagram and the answer variation in the back. Consider this combination in SAN, **1. Bg4 Qf6 2. Rxc3**. That notation paints no picture in your mind as to the combination motif. In comparison consider CRAN, **1. Bf3g4 Qf56 2. Rg3:Nc**, which reveals the motif even without a diagram (square f3 was vacated with tempo).

My personal use of CRAN during tournament play makes my score sheets easily fixable after I make notation errors or omissions. The other notated moves provide plenty of information to make corrections. In the chess960 world, notation errors might be more common because pieces reside on unfamiliar squares and have unfamiliar spatial relationships with other pieces. Using CRAN will help avoid the increase of notation or replay errors that unfamiliarity may bring.

To clarify the understanding of CRAN notation, the following table shows side-by-side comparisons of CRAN, SAN and LAN, all for White moves. When reading CRAN moves, understand that the full origin square coordinates (one letter then one digit) are always given before any other coordinates. Then the only destination square coordinates given are those that are non-redundant to the origin. The move Rf1e looks odd the first few times, just remember it begins with the origin square. Notations like e24 and Re17 are not odd looking after the first time, because only the number varies.

Piece	SAN	LAN	CRAN	Comments
♟ P				
	e4	e2-e4	e24	Why repeat 'e'?
	e5	e6-e5	e65	Dash unneeded. Minus sign reserved to annotate Black is winning. Better than "...e5".
	exf6 e.p.	e5xf6 e.p.	e5f6:f5	Bad to add two characters, lowercase 'p' and dot ('.').
	f8=Q	f7-f8=Q	f78/Q	Slash used for all extended notations. CRAN uses = only for annotation (meaning actual move was best).
♞ N				
	Ne6+	Ng5-e6+	Ng5e6#	'+' is reserved for annotating that White is winning. # means check.
♝ B				
	Bxe5	Bf4xe5	Bf4:Qe5	':' requires including type of non-pawn piece taken (even Descriptive notation gave that). 'x' clutters with column names.
♜ R				
	Rcc7	Rc3-c7	Rc37	Rcc7 is needlessly vague. Even in SAN R3c7 would be better and consume no more space.

Piece	SAN	LAN	CRAN	Comments
	Rxf7	Rc7xf7	Rc7:f	Given ':' not 'x', thus the type of piece taken is firmly implied to be P in CRAN.
	Rxf6	Rf7xf6	Rf7:N6	No repeat of 'f'.
♕ Q				
	Qd3+-	Qd1-d3+-	Qd13 +1.5	White is better by 1.5 pawns. -1.5 would mean Black is better. CRAN rejects all symbols above ASCII 0x7F, like '±'.
	Qg3#	Qd3-g3++	Qd3g##	Bad to have more types of symbols than are needed, so double the # for mate.
♔ K				
	OOO	O-O-O	Kf1c/Rbd (possible is Kc1/Rbd, or Kf1c/Rd)	Chess960 clarity. If used in chess960 OOO always means castling 'a' wing, not necessarily castling "long".

On rare occasions SAN notation is the same as CRAN. As one example, suppose a White pawn is promoted to a knight, giving White three knights on Nc8 Nc6 Ng6. For his next ply White moves his Nc6 to square e7. According to the USCF and FIDE, the officially correct SAN notation would be Nc6e7 (no dash), since anything shorter would be ambiguous. CRAN would also use Nc6e7, even if no other knights existed.

2
The Tyranny of Tradition

I confess: the first time I looked at chess960 I smirked. The initial setups looked complex and even chaotic. In those setups I perceived no structure and merely randomness. The pieces were no longer arranged symmetrically on the two wings, and they were no longer arranged by how tall each stands. This created an illusion of chaos, aided by my then still narrow experience with initial chess setups. That perceived chaos lacked appeal the same way helpmate chess puzzles composed by problemists lack appeal to me due to their unrealistic positions. Such positions, with Black's king near e4 surrounded by oddly placed pieces, do not occur in real play. After a matter of minutes I gave up on chess960 and returned to "real" chess.

One year later I was reviewing a chess game from the pages of John Nunn's superb book *Understanding Chess Move By Move*. I feel like a spectator when I review or replay a chess game, in the same way I feel like a spectator when I watch football. It was the Jan Timman – Judit Polgar game (Sigeman & Co., at Malmo 2000) in which Polgar carried an initiative through most of the opening even though Timman's moves all seemed solid and safe, even conservative. I felt like Polgar's aggressive moves were more than interesting, they were aesthetically pleasing and even inspiring. Chess is indeed a melding of war and beauty.

Then I peeked inside my one modest and aging CD of chess games, which contains about 800,000 games. This led to a feeling of deflation and almost betrayal. For I saw that the exact moves Polgar played through the opening have been played in numerous other games too. Suddenly I felt like Polgar's play had a diminished value, like that of a Picasso print as compared to a Picasso original. At that moment chess960 popped back into my head. Starting from that day I spent my evenings researching chess960, though at first I had no inkling this would lead me to write a book.

Opening Repetition Data

The problem of excessive repetition of opening moves in chess1 would be better understood by the chess public if game annotations included a marker on the first novel move of every game. In the days before the personal computer, the *Informant* series was one of the few major sources of recent important games. The majority of games were annotated with one 'N' to indicate which was the first novel move of the game. Some games broke new ground surprisingly early, such as on Black's fourth move. Most novel moves occurred much later. I decided to gather some numbers.

Using my many sided die I randomly sampled 12 games from my 1990 (#50) *Informant* from each of the main opening headings A-E, for a total of 60 games. I tallied the mean average ply which broke new ground as being ply 22.5, or plair 12. The most repetitive heading was 'D' (lots of 1. d24 d75) at 27.8 plies, or plair 14. The least repetitive was 'A' (1. c24 c75, and 1. d24 f75) at 18.3 plies, or plair 10.

I later decided to perform a similar tally for the 2005 issues of *Chess Life* I had thus far received (Jan-Aug), for the game columns of Robert Byrne and Michael Rohde. This totaled 15 games. All games were newer than any in my one aging CD of 800,000 games. For each game in *Chess Life* I followed along in the opening tree of my CD, and noted the ply at which the game was no longer in any of my opening tree branches. The mean average number of plies needed to reach novelty in the *Chess Life* games was 22.8, again plair 12.

I had been expecting the *Chess Life* games to yield a significantly higher ply count than I got from my 15 year old *Informant*. My data samples are too small, and there is not nearly enough rigor in this little data analyses to draw any firm conclusions about trends during the past 15 years. Neither *Informants* nor *Chess Life* consist of comprehensive tournament games or of randomly selected games. However it does seem that modern grandmaster games of traditional chess1 quite often begin as mere repetitions of numerous games already played, and that novelty may not appear until several plies into the middle game.

Historically, the opening phase has been considered to be the first dozen plairs, or 24 plies. In more recent chess literature there may be a tendency toward pushing that accepted boundary to perhaps the first 15 plairs. This may indicate that modern "opening" analysis has spread beyond to infect the middle game phase.

Most annotators, including Byrne and Rohde, often do not annotate the novel move of the game. My observation is that the novel move is left un-annotated in half or more of the games. Byrne commented in 4/8 of his games, Rohde commented in 2/7 of his. We might prefer a higher frequency, but at least this comment rate is higher than for all moves on average. I would like to see annotators routinely mark the novel ply of each game. Some games will have no novel move at all, but those are rarely selected for *Chess Life* publication anyway. By their sampling criteria, publishers of chess1 games will exaggerate the rate of novel opening moves.

In *Chess Life* 2005/04, Rohde made an opening annotation choice that strikes me as having an odd emphasis. The game was G.Vescovi-A.Volokitin in Bermuda 2005/02/02:

"1 e4 c5 2 Nf3 e6 3 d3 Nc6 4 g3 Nge7 5 c3
5 Bg2 g6 6 h4 had been tried by Vescovi..."

White's actual fifth ply, 5. c23, occurs only 4% of the time. Therefore it has likely not been annotated often, and perhaps not yet well. Even though Rohde breaks into text (or at least into variation) immediately after 5 c23, he never did annotate the move 5 c23 itself. Instead, Rohde chose to comment about 5. Bf1g2, which occurs in 92% of these positions. I have no trouble seeing why most White players have chosen 5. Bf1g2, but I might have benefited from Rohde explaining the reasoning behind the very uncommon 5. c23. To me, annotations of common plies in plair 5 seem less necessary than annotations of uncommon moves. To be fair, in this case Rohde was annotating Vescovi's opening tendencies, a quite relevant topic.

It must be acknowledged that a hard binary measurement of move novelty may not be the most useful for understanding the state of chess. A 25th ply recorded only twice before in a current and thorough database is still rather novel, even though not literally unique. The definition of a phrase like "has occurred often" would and should vary with context. One context is when we replay a published chess game. When I replay games of the Sicilian Defense I usually spend no time looking at the perhaps first 6 plairs. I have seen them a hundred times. I have played them myself several times. Often the annotator will have nothing to say until around the ninth plair, because the ideas are already well known.

For some chess1 games, one sad result of opening move repetition is the diminished size of the novel portion of the "organic whole". Some of the most enjoyable games to replay are those which have the longest span of novel strategies and counter measures that transmute within and through the phases of the game. When the first portion of a game duplicates exact moves we are already familiar with, the effect is to reduce the size of the novel organic whole available for us to appreciate and enjoy.

The Greatest Spectator Sport on Earth?

Is chess a 'sport'? One frequent answer is No, because it does not involve any physical skill such as eye-to-hand coordination or physical strength. Another frequent answer is Yes, it is a mind sport not an athletic sport. Personally I consider tennis to be an 'analog' sport and chess to be a 'digital' sport. A close tennis match can be a game of inches, where a player wins because his passing shot just barely caught the edge of the line for a winner. Chess is not a game of inches. There is no difference whether a knight is moved in a sloppy manner versus it being placed in the precise center of its destination square.

A digital sport like chess has at least one big advantage over an analog sport when it comes to spectators and fans: we can easily bring an old chess match back to life in our own living room any time we want. We can have it replayed at any rate of speed we want. As far as the old game itself is concerned, in digital terms we can see exactly what the famous participants saw. In contrast, even when I watch a tennis match live on television I cannot see what the players see. There is no way I can feel the power and spin of the ball against the racket by watching a replay on television. One reason is the camera angle usually chosen by broadcasters is too high above the ground. Really though, nothing short of sitting courtside can convey the speed, power, and precision of professional tennis.

The limitations of camera angle do not apply to a digital sport. The closest thing to an analog aspect of chess would be occasions where the chess clock is pressuring one of the players.

There is another strength that chess has relative to a lot of physical activities that are called sports: direct interaction between the play of the two competitors. To me direct interaction is essential for fully deserving the label of sport. The English language needs a separate word to classify physical recreations like golf, bowling, and gymnastics. Golf lacks the crucial element of direct interaction between its contestants. Golfers may walk together but they play separately. On the first day of large golf tournaments some early players end their play before others even begin. After playing a few days all the contestants simply compare their number (of strokes) to every one else's number, making it more of a contest than a competition. In gymnastics a player wins by earning a higher rating from a judge, a weakness golf avoids. *The American Heritage Dictionary* defines 'contest' as:

> "2. Any competition; especially, one in which entrants perform *separately* and are rated by judges." (italics mine)

A close score in a contest can be very exciting, but it cannot produce the same level of human drama as can the best direct interactive competition. I love golf, and I played in a golf league for many years. My feeling was of playing against my own expectations more than against anyone else or against everyone else. I get a different feeling from competing in tennis or chess, directly interacting against another person.

Compared to analog sports, digital sports have advantages of being easily captured, transmitted, and replayed. These have worked to help chess grow, albeit to the frustration of grandmasters and tournament directors who have occasionally tried to exercise copyrights over their own games.

Its digital nature has given chess a wonderful aspect that surely makes every other sport jealous: chess games stand the test of time with spectators. This very day, like every other day, perhaps ten thousand chess fans spread around the globe reviewed some old chess games. Last week I enjoyed reviewing a chess1 game between Ludek Pachman – Jiri Vesely (in Prague 1953) that occurred over a half century ago. It was not a special game like a WCC title game. The game is rarely quoted in chess literature. It is just an old game between two very good players. It would not be surprising if within 12 months from today other chess fans will also be looking at that same game. No other major sport has this same strength.

Every year America's NFL Super Bowl is one of the top two sporting events anywhere on the globe. The Super Bowl game rules the realm of television when it is live and in progress. Yet two days after the game is played it fades into forgotten history, ancient history. On cable television a sports channel occasionally shows reruns of major sporting events, including old Super Bowls and World Series baseball games. I have tried watching these on a couple of occasions. Both times it took me less than five minutes to realize those events no longer had any entertainment value for me. For you baseball fans, can you imagine every weekend wanting to watch a rerun of an old baseball game, like say the second regular season game between the Baltimore Orioles and the Kansas City Royals held during the 1974 season?

Chess fans do replay regular chess games from 1974, and from any other year you could name. So in this narrow but important sense, chess could claim to be the greatest spectator sport of all time.

Anything that harms the experience of reviewing a recent or ancient game of chess is something that should be viewed with suspicion by chess fans. This is one reason why many in the chess world expressed displeasure when in the late 1990's FIDE began to shorten the time controls in its FIDE Champion tournaments. Less thinking time means the strongest moves are found less often, and weak moves can arise to mar the game. It is also troubling to some spectators to see how repetitive the first phase of grandmaster chess1 games have become. In this respect Chess960 can offer a valuable alternative to chess spectators.

Poker Envy: In the last couple of years the gamblers' card game poker has gone from never being on television to frequently being on multiple channels at the same time. On internet chess forums we read cries of "If poker, why not chess on TV too?". I believe the basic problem with chess on television is that chess is more complex than most presentation formats can handle. It takes an insightful television producer to tame the complexity. Some have successfully handled this complexity problem, others have adjustments to make.

On July 10 2005, a chess match was played remotely, using the internet, between a Russian team and a team based in America. On July 24 the tape of the match was broadcast on various stations around America, and on some international outlets too. The show was called Chess MasterMinds. Paul Truong and Phil Innes took on the many tasks necessary to accomplish the production. In the October 2005 issue of *Chess Life*, Truong wrote about the genesis and outcome of the television program.

The format of Chess MasterMinds was to show and comment on the games in real time as the games were played. This format is similar to the format used by PBS during the WCC title match between Boris Spassky and Bobby Fischer in 1972. The Spassky-Fischer broadcasts featured one commentator displaying and analyzing the game on a demonstration board, as the moves trickled in from Iceland every few minutes. The Spassky-Fischer event was huge, so the

1972 show was a ratings success. However, the real time format may not have been so successful on Chess MasterMinds. There is sentiment that it was difficult to follow or truly understand the games while they were shown live during the program. The pace was just too fast. The problem may have been made worse by the choice of a rapid time control of Game/20 minutes. No commentator can really understand what is happening in the minds of the two players by glancing at the board between moves. Only the two players understand the game in depth while it is occurring. Others need significant study time after the game in order to absorb the depth of what was happening, or at least most spectators do.

Evidence for a Better Format: In his book *Secrets of Grandmaster Chess* (page 87), John Nunn tells of his 1975 appearance on the long running chess television show BBC Master Game. Promptly after a game ended, each player made an audio recording of himself thinking aloud. Each would record the thoughts he recalled having during each move of the game, using the present tense as if the game was currently in progress. Then the two players would re-enact their game in accordance with the producer's replaying of their spliced audio recordings. This format seems much better to me. During the broadcast, the pace of the game was restrained to the pace of the analysis. The analysis came from the highest quality source, the two players involved. The multi-year run of BBC Master Game is good evidence that many viewers liked this format.

Bobby Fischer's Perspective on FRC/Chess960

Bobby Fischer says "old chess is dead". Fischer's motivation for proposing FRC was to fix perceived problems in traditional chess. One problem Fischer dislikes is the pre-agreed grandmaster draws. With the chess1 openings known to all grandmasters, his theory is that the task of agreeing ahead of time to draw may be easier than in chess960. In 2005 on Chessville.com (and elsewhere) Susan Polgar argued well that pre-agreed draws should be viewed as part of an overall strategy to maximize a player's achievement in the tournament as a whole. Needed rest can be part of that strategy. On this narrow issue I side with Polgar. The players cannot be expected to act against their own best interests. Yet these short draws can be seen as a flaw that reduces the potential for chess on television. What would the television executives say when leading players avert an exciting finish by agreeing to non-fighting draws in the final round?

Fischer and many others prefer the ideal that no individual game should be affected by the larger context of the tournament. More importantly, the Soviets abused the concept by colluding as an unofficial team in what should have been a competition among only individuals. In any case, I see no reason to believe chess960 would prevent two players from pre-agreeing to a draw. As evidence I submit the following game from the final round of the Chess Tigers FiNet Chess960 Open held in Mainz, Germany in August 2005. The elite top ten grandmaster Levon Aronian needed only a draw to win the tournament for his second time in his latest two tries.

L.Aronian – R.Lanka, R#708-S#651 RNKR-BQNB

1.	f24	f75	2.	g23	g76	3.	d23	d76
4.	e24	Be8c6	5.	Nb1c3	e76	6.	Be1d2	Nb8d7
7.	Ng1e2	.5-.5						

Another problem Fischer dislikes is that most grandmaster chess1 games begin with a long repetition of moves that have already been played in many earlier games. Fischer sees this and pronounces that old chess is "played out". The majority of grandmasters disagree, but not all.

During his 2004 WCC title defense match against challenger Peter Leko, Vladimir Kramnik described his belief that short draws in chess were inevitable because the openings have been so heavily analyzed. Jack Peters, the renowned chess columnist for the *Los Angeles Times*, perhaps light-heartedly argued that Kramnik was at least partly incorrect:

> "[Kramnik's] opening preparation extended all the way to a slightly inferior endgame that Black is supposed to be able to draw. Leko won anyway. Chess is not exhausted yet!"

Kramnik's home analysis has become so penetrating that he correctly predicted a precise endgame position that occurred during the match. It happened there was a flaw in Kramnik's analysis of how that endgame would progress. Peters seemed to argue that Kramnik's endgame analysis flaw shows chess1 is not yet exhausted. But that line of reasoning focuses on the secondary aspect. I find much more compelling the primary fact that Kramnik correctly predicted the endgame position. It suggests the opposite conclusion, that chess1 is partially exhausted to an unpleasant and unsporting degree.

The effects of extreme opening analysis are usually thought to have consumed only the opening phase of chess1. In reality the problem of repetitious opening moves has spread to infect the middle game too. The problem is demonstrated when authors can describe the "main line" firmly into the middle game at plair 15 (*Play the Sicilian Dragon* by Edward Dearing, ch. 9, 15 f4). When I see a novel middle game move annotated with verbiage exclaiming such moves prove chess is not exhausted, my reaction is the opposite. Chess1 must indeed be partially exhausted if such a late arrival of novelty is cause for cheer.

Alexei Shirov's *Fire on the Board* contains a chapter "The Botvinnik Variation" about Shirov's play in games featuring the Semi-Slav Defense. John Watson referred to that chapter in his own book *Secrets of Modern Chess Strategy: Advances Since Nimzowitsch* (page 226):

> "The remarkable but typical thing about these games is that, although they often diverge from preparation only at a *late* stage (say, move 18 or 20), they are consistently full of rich and unforeseeable complications. ... This paradox, that *deeply*-prepared variations can produce incredibly creative over-the-board contests, manifests itself time and again in contemporary chess." (italics mine)

Everyone is genuinely glad that variety can emerge in chess1 after the repetitious opening and middle game plies are reproduced, around plair 18 or 20. I take Watson's point to be that the post-repetition variety is not slight, that it branches out to a tree as rich as what we would expect from an early opening position. All good, if true. Yet this does not mean chess1 can produce as wide a variety of logical play and positions as can chess960. Nor does this mean the average plair count of a chess1 game is growing along with the growing penetration of home analysis into the middle game. If a given game becomes decisive around plair 40, but the first 18 plairs were a repetition of numerous games already studied, then the present game provided 22 plairs of top quality entertainment for spectators. In chess960 most games would provide closer to 40 plairs of entertainment. Novelty is desirable, and chess1 shortens and delays novelty. Ultimately it is a matter of degree, but I say novelty delayed is novelty denied.

It is presumed these problems in chess1 will continue to get worse. No other outcome even seems possible. With the emergence of the powerful personal computer and chess databases around 1990, the growth of these problems accelerated. During the last 10-15 years there has been an explosion in the at-home calculations of opening variations. Novelties are sometimes planned for moves like White's 23rd and even later. Is that sporting competition, or is that at least partly puzzle solving at home? Click your way through any chess opening tree built from actual games and you will see that the vast majority of games are mere repeats of many other games into the middle game. The database numbers do not lie.

Foreseeing Better Chess1 Opening Annotations Using Statistics: The highest quality form of annotation will always the explanatory sentence. Yet by around the year 2060, the repetitious state of chess1 could be so strained that the proper way to annotate games may evolve. Reliable win/loss ratio statistics for White could be given frequently during a variation, even after every ply for the first 20 plairs. This is not to imply that grandmasters will have played every possible variation through 20 plairs numerous times. But eventually games that veer out of oft recorded variations will likely be exceptionally weak for one color or the other (that being why they are rare).

During the 1900's, authors of opening books usually rated each opening variation with a vague symbol such as "+-" or "±" or "=", to indicate merely the degree to which White has the better position. This practice remains prevalent today. For longer opening variations, an annotator today could site the evaluation from a strong computer chess program doing its own calculation based assessment. This would be in the now familiar units of pawns, such as +.4 to indicate White stands better by almost a half pawn. This kind of number is more specific than is "+-", but the accuracy of its source, and even its proper interpretation, will always be in some doubt. Eventually there will be a higher quality annotation option.

Future opening annotators will use Chess Database 2060 to provide the highly relevant empirical statistic of White's win/loss ratio for most variations, indeed for most plies. For the variations that account for 80% of grandmaster games, the White win/loss ratio will be between 1.35 and 1.00. There is a big difference between the ratios of 1.14 and 1.06.

Even today this ratio could be used for the most common variations, such as those discussed in the "Starting Out" series of opening books published by Everyman. But those books do not provide the win/loss ratio. Even the dense opening books published by Gambit omit the ratio information, even though the books are aimed at stronger players. However, the ratio is given in the book *Master the Spanish* by Daniel King and Pietro Ponzetto. That is only one way in which their book is unusual.

None of this is to imply that computers are hurting chess. Quite the opposite. The 2005 FIDE Chess Champion Veselin Topalov believes computers are the reason young players are achieving grandmaster titles at ever earlier ages (*Chess Life*, December 2005, pg 16). Computers are not hurting chess. Computers are advancing chess beyond the limits of chess1.

Planning is Cool, Solving is Stale: Clever advance planning is pleasing to watch when it helps win in an analog sport. It was thrilling in the 1980's when the NFL San Francisco 49er's, under head coach Bill Walsh, began their successful offensive attacks based on play sequences scripted before the game. The novelty was that Walsh stuck to the scripted play sequence regardless of how the previous plays went. Thrills came from knowing quarterback Joe Montana still had to throw the ball to a precise spot so that Jerry Rice could catch it a fleeting moment before the defender converged to tackled Rice. Planning did not perform those physically demanding tasks where inches and half-seconds were the essence. Chess of course is not a game of inches, and there is no execution aspect beyond the script. The dignity of any digital sport is at risk if home planning can become too specific and can penetrate too deeply into an individual game. Bill Walsh planned his opening plays. Grandmasters are solving the chess1 openings.

Fischer's common thread is that chess960 would fix some of the problems inherent in chess1. When I began to think about chess960 my first thoughts were in accordance with Fischer's perspective. After I thought more deeply about chess960 my own perspective shifted away from Fischer's. For me the issue of repetitious openings and middle games in chess1 remains important, yet it has fallen to secondary status. I have come to believe there are even better reasons all chess players should want to give chess960 an honest chance.

Learning From the Checkers Example

Checkers (or draughts) is a sport with a very long history. The first World Champion of checkers was crowned in 1847, four decades before Steinitz and Zukertort declared their match to be for the world title. In Scotland Andrew Anderson defeated James Wyllie in that first title match. Fifty years later checkers was facing the same crisis of played out openings that Fischer emphasizes is upon us now in chess1. In checkers the problem was more severe. To their credit the influential people in checkers took decisive action to alleviate the problem, and they changed the rules of their venerable game, tradition notwithstanding.

See if this sounds familiar. Around 1900 a new rule was implemented in checkers to randomly choose from among a set of acceptable initial setups. This was called the 2-Move rule (using move in the sense of ply). Around 1934 the rule was strengthened to become the 3-Move rule. Today the 3-Move rule defines 156 acceptable initial setups. A special deck of cards has been designed to randomly choose from among the valid setups.

The 3-Move rule set for checkers seems extremely similar to the chess960 idea. Maybe they should use the name checkers156!   The original rule of checkers, allowing unrestricted opening moves from the same one position, also survives to this day. It is called Unrestricted or GAYP (go-as-you-please) checkers. Unrestricted checkers is highly analogous to chess1. In the checkers world nobody calls the 3-Move rule set a "variant" of Unrestricted checkers, nor the reverse. They are called different "styles" of checkers. The checkers world does have two world champion titles, one for each rule set. In fact, checkers aficionado Jim Loy reports that the title of World Champion in 3-Move checkers has become more prestigious than the title of WC in Unrestricted checkers. Loy also reports that 3-Move is more common in serious checkers tournaments than is Unrestricted, and that it leads to fewer draws. The 2005 3-Move World Championship of checkers match had a draw rate of only 25/36 = 69.4%, less than the 10/14 = 71.4% from the 2004 WCC title match between Kramnik and Leko. These draw rates look great compared to checkers title matches in the 1800's in which half the Unrestricted games were identical, not merely drawn. The tremendous success of the 3-Move rule in checkers raises a reasoned challenge to chess1 devotees who feel chess960 has nothing positive to offer the chess world.

More Checkers Similarities: In 2001 the reigning 3-Move champion was Ron "Suki" King, of Barbados. King had his title taken away by some of the major checkers organizations Many felt King was endlessly haggling over the details of his title defense, and that the situation had become unreasonable (deja vu). The challenger, Alex Moiseyev of the USA by way of Russia, was assigned an alternative opponent whom he defeated to become the 3-Move world champion. The checkers world champion title was then split because some other checkers organizations said it was improper to take away King's title by declaration. To me checkers would seem more prone to this split title problem than is chess, because the strongest checkers organizations are national not international. Thus checkers has multiple organizations sharing or fighting for the top rung.

My impression from my own childhood is that more American children play checkers at least one time than play chess at least one time. Checkers has its heroes too. Marion Tinsley (1927-1995) was the greatest checkers player ever to walk the Earth. His perch at the top spanned five decades and it was not diminished by old age. His dominance was so thorough that from 1951 through 1993 Tinsley won every tournament he played in, never even sharing first place, losing about one game per decade. Nobody in chess history can compare on the same scale, not even Andre Philidor or Paul Morphy. Mr. Tinsley was by every account an exceptionally friendly gentleman. Any sport would dream to have someone like Tinsley as its representative. Cancer took Tinsley shortly after he had the pleasure of playing a computer program named Chinook that could finally give him a real fight. Tinsley won his 1992 match against Chinook +4-2=33.

Impedance to Rejoining the USCF

Fischer has described the damage he believes the limited chess1 opening phase is doing to grandmaster chess. There may be drawbacks at the club level as well. In chess forums on the web, a portion of the chess960 discussion is about how dull some players find the task of "memorizing opening moves". Adults with busy lives post comments saying they want to get back into tournament chess. But they are hesitant because they feel discouraged knowing they no longer remember how to play the openings as well as when they had lots of time to dedicate to chess. Searching the web I had no trouble gathering examples similar to the following from a man in his 40's who was a class

A player twenty years ago (from Bruce Pandolfini's column *The Q & A Way* on ChessCafe.com, 2005/04):

> "Any recommendations on how to approach opening preparation when one has little time to study massive amounts of theory and learn tons of lines?"

In his reply the master recommended studying from software over physical paper books, and the testing of openings in Blitz games. Here is another part of the master's reply:

> "Play over hundreds of critically current games. See which variations suit you."

I wonder whether the busy player was happy with that part, though I am not suggesting there is a better answer.

Other web postings ask about openings that require the least amount of opening memorization. They seek one opening that can be used against any first move by White or against any replies by Black. There are several opening books available that are marketed by explicitly targeting this type of adult player, because it is recognized that many chess1 players are worried about their opening preparations. I think the concerns of these players are overblown for club level play. But perception can create reality, so their concerns are real. I believe there are adults across the country who do not return to the USCF and tournament chess partly because of their discomfort with the chess1 opening phase.

Chess960 a Partial Solution: Would adults who dislike some aspects of the chess1 opening phase be more inclined to rejoin the USCF and tournament play if chess960 were part of the scene? As I stated earlier, the USCF should establish for every member a rating eligible for chess960 results. I would strongly recommend against a separate rating and its attending fragmentation, because a class B player in chess1 will end up as a class B player in chess960. Both are just chess. But it is likely some USCF members would object to affecting the primary chess1 rating with chess960 results, though I am not clear on why. There would be only a harmless minuscule effect on the standard ratings if chess960 proves unpopular and only a few people play a few chess960 games. If chess960 does prove to be popular then it will be affirmed that the USCF did the right thing by meeting the desires of its membership. Either way the rating numbers themselves will not go up or down by the addition of chess960.

Befuddled By Time Data

I have twice won the monthly contest in the *Chess Life* column of Larry Evans. My most recent prize was a copy of Evans' book *The 10 Most Common Chess Mistakes...and How to Avoid Them!* On his page 215 Evans wrote:

> "The Ruy Lopez is so heavily analyzed that both sides often rattle off a series of book moves that land them in the middle game before they know it. The Breyer Defense has been repeated in countless games..."

Having said so much about semi-exhausted openings, it can be humorous and maybe informative to note how chess clock readings look when written next to plies on a game move score sheet. From *Jon Speelman's Best Games* we have some far too rare notations that include clock readings. Speelman's clock notations reveal that even memorized opening moves are not always played rapidly the way the word 'memorized' makes it seem. We find examples like this (page 69):

J.Speelman – M.Stean, London 1980

1.	d24	(0:03)	Ng8f6	(0:00)
2.	c24	(0:04)	e76	(0:00)
3.	Ng1f3	(0:08)	b76	(0:01)
4.	Nb1c3	(0:11)	Bc8b7	(0:03)
5.	Bc1g5	(0:14)	h76	(0:11)
6.	Bg5h4	(0:16)	g75	(0:12)
7.	Bh4g3	(0:16)	Nf6h5	(0:12)

Finally with his seventh ply Speelman makes an early game move in under 60 seconds. Are we to conclude that Speelman was thrown by Black's wild unforeseeable second move? Does it take four minutes to play a memorized move, for only your third ply? Even for subsequent moves like the risky Ng1f3 and the daring Bc1g5, Speelman never took less than three minutes.

I would guess Speelman was using the time to decide which available variation he felt more comfortable pursuing given all the circumstances. How frequently has Stean seen or played the different variations? How well does Speelman himself remember the sub-variations? What mood is he in, and so on. As a former WCC candidate, Jon Speelman in his prime was an elite among grandmasters. Speelman was not trying to remember "Oh gosh, now what is White supposed to play here on move three, I am pretty sure I have seen this opening before, if I could just remember...".

At the opposite end of the spectrum there are cases like Garry Kasparov's famous victory in game 10 of his 1995 WCC title defense match against challenger Vishy Anand. During match preparations Kasparov had devised a variation deep into the middle game wherein he would sacrifice an exchange on his 21st ply. Kasparov would give up a rook to recapture Anand's bishop. Kasparov had further pre-calculated a tactical win for himself after the sacrifice. Anand's moves in game 10 were exactly as Kasparov had predicted, giving Kasparov the opportunity to spring his sacrifice and win. It took Kasparov only 6 minutes to play his complex 21 plies up to the sacrifice. From there Kasparov went on to the victory he had foreseen. In the Speelman game at the 6 minute mark, Jon would use another 2 minutes to decide that 3. Ng1f3 follows d24 c24.

So Kasparov successfully predicted the first 21 plairs of a hard fought game in a short title match. This illuminates the issues with the heavily analyzed chess1 openings in a way that aggregate statistics cannot. It is one thing to find the same game through the first 21 plairs when searching a database during post-mortem. It is quite another to correctly predict the first 21 plairs of a match game only days or weeks before the prediction proves accurate. At one level this correct prediction was fascinating, and at another it was horrifying. Most chess1 games in which the opening moves are entirely foreseen lack the exciting punch of this Kasparov-Anand gem. For better or worse, such a prediction could never happen in chess960.

An Optimistic Perspective on Chess960

"Old chess" is not dead, nor will it ever die, nor should it die. Chess1 should flourish. Chess960 is not about changing the rules of chess1. Chess960 is about recognizing that chess1 is a subset of Caissa's full chess. Chess1 is the small visible part of the whole chess iceberg. A large portion of chess lies hidden below the surface, as chess960. We cannot experience the fullness of pure chess if we limit ourselves to chess1 exclusively.

Chess960 is about having an even richer chess experience than chess1 traditions have delivered.

During the Renaissance, astronomers using spectroscopy realized our Sun is not unique but is rather just one among billions of similar stars. This changed the way humanity perceived the world, both scientifically and spiritually. The Sun was not changed by that discovery any more than our recognition of chess960 changes chess1. But I can no longer feel the chess1 setup to be any more deserving or interesting than the other 959 setups. In my view, when the ancients invented modern chess and chess1, they simultaneously created chess960. Chess960 is almost the same as chess1. The games seen as forerunners of modern chess1 suffered from archaic bishops (required to move exactly two squares), from weakling queens and thus weaker pawns, and so were only superficially like chess1. In 1475 chess1 was not revised, it was invented. Like most inventions, chess1 was a logical incremental step forward from what preceded it. Very few inventions borrow nothing from the earlier work of others.

I have come to see the traditional static setup as a contrivance. This is most obvious in its wing symmetry feature (each wing has RNB), as wing symmetry is uncommon among all chess960 setups. Setups with wing symmetry naturally provide less variety of play than do other individual setups. This is ironic because the static nature of the chess1 setup already embodies a major impedance to variety compared to chess960. As will be discussed later, the legacy rule that the king castling to the 'a' wing ends two squares from the protective edge, versus only one square away for 'h' wing castling, constricts variety even further. When variety is restricted, increased repetition must result. We see the same B-N5 pin-the-knight maneuver on both wings, and it is inherent in the chess1 setup. But there are hundreds of chess960 setups that do not facilitate this maneuver on either wing, and extremely few that facilitate it so easily on both wings. The chess1 queen just happens to be ideally set up in the center for protecting pieces in the early game. In chess1 we often find we cannot move our Qd1 diagonally to position it in front of the opponent's castled king (on g4 or h5), due to the repetitious positioning of the opposing Nf6. This particular tactical relationship between pressure and counter-pressure, between Qd1 and Ng8 at square g4, is inherent in the chess1 setup. Both bishops are placed so they can be developed without needing prior advancement of the wing pawns needed for a secure post-castling king fort. The knights just happen to start on squares that make it as easy as possible to reach their ideal development squares of c3 f3. With Nf3 we see one of the very few standard post-castling king forts chess1 produces. So limited and repetitious are the chess1 king forts that books have been written covering all the ways each king fort can be attacked.

By endlessly reusing only one setup, chess1 forever hides from us the many interesting strategic and tactical issues that arise from the other 959 setups. We noted a few of the tactical and positional themes inherent in the chess1 setup. Is the chess1 setup the only one that has inherent themes?: of course not. Chess players should recognize that all the other chess960 setups offer their own kinds of chess themes, but that chess1 players rarely or never get to experience those themes. As just one instance, the effects can be intellectually stimulating when the two knights start on unfamiliar squares, especially on squares of the same shade for a change. I have seen several writers derisively dismiss the whole chess960 concept. However, not one of those critics has yet explained why the new strategic and tactical issues arising from chess960 should be uninteresting to chess players. My impression is that some critics are not fully aware of these new elements, forcing me to question whether their derogatory writings about chess960 are a service or a disservice to their readers.

New Ways of Studying the Opening: A common statement about chess960 is that grandmasters devoted to chess960 would not have to study the openings. The theory is that since there is vastly more to learn about the opening phase in chess960 that there is no point in even trying. A corollary implication is that grandmasters would never improve their opening play in chess960, an assertion I find unrealistic.

My guess is that chess960 grandmasters would study the opening phase, but not with the old chess1 technique. The traditional approach to opening study, with its learning and retention of very specific ideas (or of move trees), would not apply to chess960. So new ways to study the opening would have to be invented. The 960 setups in chess960 may seem endlessly diverse and complex, much like all the possible middle game positions are. Yet I believe the chess960 setups are less diverse than they seem at first. Firstly, it is closer to the truth to say there are only 480 setups, even though due to the traditional asymmetry in the castling rule that is technically false. Secondly, in strategic terms and in some tactical terms, each setup has similarities with many others, and these similarities can be recognized and leveraged.

These opening phase ideas will be discussed in detail in a later chapter. I bring them up here to make a point about another drawback of chess1 relative to chess960. In 1984 the first WCC title match between champion Anatoly Karpov and challenger Garry Kasparov turned into an embarrassing spectacle when it dragged on for months with draw after draw. Though ahead 5 wins to 3, Karpov was near physical and thus mental collapse. This compelled FIDE to step in and declare the match over with the infamous "no result". I doubt it was the daytime games that eroded Karpov's health. I suspect it was the nightly opening preparations for tomorrow's games that did the damage. In chess960 tournaments the players can go to bed early, guilt free. The old eliminated policy of having adjourned games was disliked because it caused this same sleep deprivation that is still caused by chess1 openings.

In chess1, at the level of candidate matches and up, the kind of opening study that is needed often resembles the kind of pre-test cramming that college students do. Grandmasters focus their opening study on the recent opening play of their expected opponents. This is very different from the kind of opening study that would be needed to become WCC in a highly competitive chess960 world. Chess960 opening study would be more like endgame study. After playing all day no grandmaster has to stay up late preparing for things like the N+P+P versus B+P endgame. Any grandmaster could always tune up his endgame skills at the margin, but there is no pressure to cram when sleep would be recommended.

Chess Publishers and Retailers Would Benefit From Adding Chess960: The highest selling group of chess books is targeted at children or beginners. But for adult customers, openings books are the most reliable source of revenue for chess book publishers. Publishers may feel their business would be reduced if chess960 were to co-exist with chess1. Players may feel there would be no point to buying an excellent book on the strongest variations in chess960 setup number 412 even if such a book could be compiled. There is no way to know when or even if you would ever play a game with that setup. The ChessBase company may feel the opening tree databases they sell would be useless in a chess960 world. I suspect these conjectures would turn out to be false. I would not be surprised if all kinds of chess publishers benefited from chess960 rising to brotherhood with chess1.

It seems axiomatic that the new opening phase of chess960 would demand a whole new set of books to discover and teach how to best play the new phase. Some of those books could take the approach of devising opening principles. Others could focus on one non-traditional setup and give us a feel for its possibilities. That setup analysis could then be compared and contrasted to analysis known in chess1, providing a valuable perspective unavailable today. Play from actual tournament games could be compiled, and computer programs like ChessBase and Fritz9 could help build a modest opening tree for the non-traditional setup. Humanity has deeply assessed only one of the 960 setups. We have no measure of variability until we have at least two setups deeply measured, so we can compare.

In chess960 the goal for each student will be to develop an intuitive feel for how to approach setups with different kinds of attributes. Closely examining a variety of setups should help foster that intuition. This kind of study would be free from the drudgery often associated with memorizing and retaining specific variations as in chess1.

Would Reshevsky Have Been WCC?:   The opening phase difference in chess960 might have been an advantage to some noted players in history. The case of Samuel Reshevsky comes to mind. FIDE held a WCC title tournament in Amsterdam in 1948, to fill the vacancy left by the death of WCC Alexander Alekhine (al-YEKK-inn) in 1946. Reshevsky competed, but the tournament was won by Mikhail Botvinnik. Reshevsky had a particular reputation as a player highly skilled at navigating the opening phase without benefit of deeply memorized opening lines. Botvinnik was the complete opposite, as the father of the Soviet school that elevated opening preparation to a rigorous relentless science (much to Botvinnik's credit). Botvinnik thus had the opening phase as an advantage over Reshevsky. I suspect Reshevsky might have won this 1948 tournament and the WCC title if the rule set had been chess960. Botvinnik would have been forced to figure out openings in real time during the games, something Reshevsky did routinely even in chess1.

Center of the Universe for FRC/Chess960

Chess960 has only a tiny following today in 2005, though I believe its popularity is growing.   In the late 1990's Bobby Fischer could have promoted chess960 with the considerable force of his then still exalted status in the chess world.   Instead to outsiders like me it seems Fischer played games of chess960 just in his living room when visitors were arranged.   It was left to others to do the hard work necessary to breathe life into the chess960 concept.

Enter Hans-Walter Schmitt.   Mr. Schmitt leads the Chess Tigers organization based in Mainz, Germany (ChessTigers.de). Fischer became the creator of chess960 in 1996 by making insightful refinements to the historical ideas of others.   To me it seems history should record Schmitt as a "co-founder" of chess960. Schmitt has obtained sponsors (including FiNet and Livingston) and organized a large annual August chess event that includes rapid tournaments of both chess1 and chess960 (time controls are Game/20 minutes +5 seconds delay).   This chess960 tournament has consistently drawn many of the biggest names in chess.   World Chess1 Championship challenger Peter Leko has been involved. Several other world top ten rated players have been involved including Michael Adams, Alexei Shirov, FIDE champions Rustam Kazimdzhanov and Ruslan Ponomariov, Peter Svidler, Levon Aronian, and Entienne Bacrot. Many others from the current or past FIDE top 25 list play chess960 in Mainz.   The famous names include Alexandra Kosteniuk, Antoaneta Stefanova, Yasser Seirawan, Vlastimil Hort, Artur Yusupov, Rafael Vaganian, and 2004 winner Zoltan Almasi (Almasi lost the title match to defending champion Svidler in August 2005).   The Mainz chess960 tournament has earned the respect of everyone. Mainz   has become the center of the universe for chess960.   A chess1 tournament is held in Mainz during the same week.   But the Mainz participants know it is their pioneering chess960 tournament that has gained world wide attention. Future chess historians will perpetuate the memory of Mainz for its chess960 tournament.

What are Chess, Chess1, and Chess960?

What is Chess?: Before this book can put ideas into their proper unbiased relations to each other, we need to reconsider the name 'chess'. In this book the term 'chess' is considered a general or generic term for any rule set that honorably implements the pure intentions of Caissa (kahh-EE-sahh), the goddess daughter of Mars and Aphrodite (war and beauty), the adopted muse of chess. This includes the square shaped board perfectly sized at 8x8. It also includes the well known six types of pieces and their modern rules of movement. But it does not have to include the less important rule that makes stalemate a draw instead of a win. Nor must it include exactly c1 and g1 as being the only king destination squares for White castling. Nor must it include the in-passing rule for pawn capture. Andre Philidor believed a pawn could be promoted only to a type of piece already taken by the enemy, but I would say Philidor was still a chess player. A rule set could possibly still qualify as chess even though it differed with a minor rule or two. The traditional rule set, firmly in place by the 1830's and the era of Howard Staunton, currently is the prevailing implementation of chess. But by no means is it the only possible legitimate implementation of chess. If pawns were never allowed to advance more than one square per move, our game would still be chess. Now if bishops were required to move exactly two squares, that would not be chess.

Fairy chess, Bughouse chess and Janus chess would not qualify as true chess games. Those variants of chess deviate too dramatically from the fundamental ideas underlying chess. For instance, any increase in board size drastically relaxes the crucial cramping aspect of chess.

Speedier Pawn, But Why?: After modern chess was invented in 1475, its pawn was allowed to advance only one square even on its first move. Later the pawn was empowered to advance two squares, though only the first time it moved. Why was this rule change made? The historians I have read all use the word 'speed'. They say vaguely that with the faster game of the highly mobile bishop and queen, the feeling was the game would benefit from the higher speed of a two square pawn move. I doubt speeding the game was the primary motivation. Instead I suspect they repeatedly saw the new long range bishop move to pin an enemy knight with B-N5 (such as Bc1g5), and that they felt this maneuver was too common and too uncontestable. By giving the pawn the two square advance option, they enabled pawns to coordinate together to break the pin by the enemy bishop (B-N5, P-R3, B-R4, P-N4, B-N3).

Now consider the relationship between the initial setup and the B-N5 pin. Compared to the other chess960 setups, the chess1 setup is extraordinarily conducive to enabling this general maneuver. Other setups facilitate this same conceptual B-pins-N maneuver on only one wing, with Bb1f5. Other setups seem to not facilitate it much at all. Aside from the traditional R#362 and its reciprocal R#862, I wonder whether there is any other setup that so thoroughly facilitate B pins N? The modern pawn might have never had any two square advance option had the inventors in 1475 chosen either RBNQ-KNBR or the chess960 rule set.

The Difference Between an Implementation Versus a Variant of Chess: Not all proposed rule sets are as true to Caissa's spirit as are the best rule sets. At some imperfectly definable point, a rule set seems to stray too far to deserve being considered an implementation of chess. Instead it becomes a variant of chess.

The most popular variant of chess is Blitz chess. Is variant too harsh a term in describing Blitz? The extremely brief time control of Game-in-5-minutes per player is merely an off-the-board rule difference from normal tournament chess. Yet its effects throughout the whole game are severe, and that is one proper criterion for judging a variant. In 2005 a person posting on the USCF web site forum put it this way:

> "Blitz in general is a completely different form of chess in which the time element actually takes precedence over the game."

Indeed, an off-the-board rule change can have a bigger effect than some on-the-board rule changes. Jonathan Maxwell wrote a chess book entitled *Blitz Theory*. The book is devoted to the special strategies involved in winning at Blitz chess:

> "The game of blitz chess is only a *relative* of slow chess, as blitz is chess within a time crisis." *(From the Introduction, italics mine.)*

An off-the-board rule change can cause a bigger change from chess than some on the board rule changes. If other readers feel that label of variant is too extreme for Blitz, I will not quibble. For me the inner experiences I feel while playing Blitz bear little resemblance to those I feel from playing chess with a traditional slow time control. For me personally, this difference is so big that Blitz feels like a variant of chess.

Removing Blitz and chess960 from the discussion for a moment, the most popular variant of chess seems to be Bughouse chess. In 2005 I have seen four tournament announcements that mention a side event of Bughouse. With its dual boards, human teammates, and return to action for taken pieces, I doubt anyone would deny the label of 'variant' applies to Bughouse. Chess960 is nothing like Bughouse or the other earlier mentioned variants. Side events at major tournaments are a common way to make these other types of chess tournaments available. Perhaps chess960 will gain entry into American chess via the side event route. Independently of me, in November 2005 the organizers of the annual Washington State Class Championship tournament did exactly that.

First In Wins

According to an article in the Seattle Times newspaper (2005/03/25), Japanese educators were concerned that ever fewer students were joining the sumo wrestling teams. The educators made a plea for a rule change in junior level sumo wrestling. They asked that student athletes be allowed to wear tight bicycle pants during wrestling matches instead of the traditional but immodest mawashi thong. The powers governing sumo wrestling were emphatic in their refusal to consider the proposal. Tradition was used to trump what many see as a common sense change.

I believe the sense of tradition is a primary reason there is resistance to chess960 in the chess1 community. Had those who invented chess in 1475 chosen the chess960 rule set, I believe most of the chess players who today resist or ignore chess960 would instead be resisting any chess1 proposals. Thus their preference is not determined by any objective assessment of the differing advantages of the two rule sets, rather their preference is determined by what other people have said and done, and by what they were born into.

The Other Way Around: Let us imagine the histories of chess1 and chess960 were reversed, and that those who re-implemented chess in 1475 had included the chess960 setup randomization along with all the more radical rule changes they decreed. Had that happened, chess960 would today be the norm dating back centuries. Now add to our imagination that a great chess player is today proposing a rule change away from chess960 to a new game chess1:

"We should pick exactly one of the 960 setups and use only that one in all of our chess games. The other 959 setups we have been playing should be permanently forbidden in rated games. This way grandmasters could study and memorize the best opening moves for all branches from that one setup. As tournament results accumulate we could publish books and databases showing which opening moves lead to the best win percentages. Over time the best variations would be learned ever deeper into the game, past the opening and into the middle game. This will lead to a weeding out of inferior opening moves as players repeat the best moves published thus far. That means the grandmaster community will have achieved a higher quality of play, thus making games better for chess enthusiasts to replay for enjoyment.

Which one setup should be chosen? The ideal setup should have a visually pretty appearance on the board, probably through some sort of symmetry. The knights should be placed where they can easily reach their ideal squares c3 f3 or c6 f6 with a single move. We should place the queen on a central column."

In our imagined world of traditional chess960, this proposal would have been met with enormous resistance. It would represent a massive loss in the range and beauty of the entire opening phase of chess. It would also harm the middle game phase (as we shall see). The resistance to chess1 would be more severe than is the resistance to chess960 in the real world today. I feel that difference tells us something positive about the merits of chess960 when tradition is excluded as a factor.

Yet there would be one important selling point in the argument for inclusion of chess1: the static nature of the chess1 setup has led to a higher quality of opening play than we would get from chess960. Since higher quality play is generally more enjoyable to spectators, this is an advantage chess1 has over chess960. Unfortunately, the heavy price for that higher quality has proven to be a great deal of opening repetition, and a loss of some interesting middle game variety that belongs as part of chess proper.

Back now in the real world, we can foresee a day when grandmaster chess960 tournaments might no longer be rare. As those games begin to accumulate in the latest databases, we will be judging the quality of play. The razor sharp opening play of chess1 will have given us a valuable benchmark of what constitutes superb opening play, making us better able to judge how well chess960 openings are being played.

During the 21st century I expect the argument for chess960 will eventually gain the respect of a critical mass of chess players and chess authorities. For now what people judge to be the better rule set for chess is based less on merit and more on the limited range of their experiences and what they grew up with. I call this the "tyranny of tradition". This book is urging readers to give more weight to merit over tradition in assessing chess960. The USCF should formally recognize chess960.

Opening Theme Tournaments

Occasionally we hear about an opening theme chess1 tournament being held. In such tournaments all players agree beforehand that all games will start with the same first few moves. A theme tournament might have all games begin 1. e24 c75 2. c23, with Black then to choose his next move as in a typical game. Games from such tournaments have been included in the same formal player ratings by the USCF. The USCF rule book says nothing directly about this policy, but a USCF official has explicitly said and re-confirmed the rating of theme games is acceptable. Also, USCF members have reported that games from their theme tournaments were indeed rated (UsChess.org forum, 2005).

To my mind chess1 is a theme tournament run amok in what should be a chess960 world. For entertainment purposes only, let us look at whether and how the theme tournament concept could make possible some ratable games of chess960. Consider a chess1 theme tournament where all games began:

1.	e23	e76	2.	Qd1f3	Qd8f6	3.	Bf1e2	Bf8e7
4.	Be2d1	Be7d8	5.	Ng1e2	Ng8e7	6.	Ne2g3	Ne7g6
7.	Qf3e2	Qf6e7	8.	Qe2f1	Qe7f8	9.	Qf1g	Qf8g
10.	Ng3f1	Ng6f8	11.	(any)				
		(D2.1)						

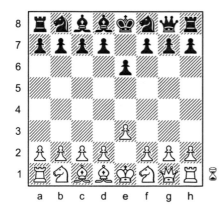

D2.1
After chess1 theme ply 10... Ng6f8.

White's next move is discretionary.

Very similar to chess960 R#745.

55

This arrives at a setup that is very nearly R#745-S#549 RNBB-KNQR in chess960. R#745 has not yet occurred in Mainz (nor has its reciprocal R#245).

3
Formalizing the Rules of Chess960

This chapter begins with a formal statement of the chess rule set named FRC. The FRC rule set captures a moment in history, June 19 1996, when Bobby Fischer announced his one proposed rule change. FRC is therefore considered to be unchangeable by definition. Later sections of this chapter progress from FRC to chess960. The informal description Bobby Fischer gave of FRC left some important formalities unaddressed. Later sections of this chapter will address those gaps.

I have also included a few editorial comments at the start of some sections. The chess960 rule set retains the eligibility to evolve further, if the consensus so desires. In a subsequent chapter I will propose a few more significant rule improvements for chess960.

The FRC Rule Set

Rule A1: Legacy chess rules continue by default.

All the rules of chess1 apply to the FRC rule set unless otherwise stated.

Rule A2: Notation.

1. FRC requires algebraic notation exclusively. No form of old descriptive notation is acceptable.

2. Proper score sheet notation requires that the initial setup be recorded before the game starts. This can be done with a piece setup string. For example, the setup string format could be RNBQ-KBNR for the traditional chess1 setup, in sequence of column 'a' to 'h'.

Rule A3: Initial Setup and Validation.

The initial setup of the pieces is usually different in FRC from chess1. The FRC setup rule is described below.

1. The eight White pawns fill row 2, and their Black counterparts fill row 7.

2. The eight White non-pawn pieces fill row 1, and their Black counterparts fill row 8.

3. The two White bishops must be on different shade squares from each other, one on light the other on dark.

4. The White king must be between the two White rooks.

5. Each White and Black piece must be of the same type as its counterpart at the other end of its column, in mirror fashion. For example, if the White king is setup on square f1, the Black king must be setup on f8.

6. Within these constraints, all 960 possible setups must have an equal chance of being randomly selected for the game.

7. Neither player should know the randomly selected setup until roughly ten minutes before the game begins.

Rule A4: Unbiased Castling Rule.

In the official USCF chess1 rule book from 1987, the castling rules consume over four pages. Too many of the FRC castling rule formulations I have seen are unnecessarily long and complex. The castling rule for FRC is fundamentally the same as in chess1, and every formulation of the FRC castling rule covers the chess1 case also.

1. It is given that the king must reside between his two rooks in the initial setup.

2. Castling is a single ply that involves the movement of two pieces of the same color, primarily the king, and secondarily a chosen rook. A castling is always considered to have moved both the king and rook, even though in some castling moves the king or chosen rook may have been initially set up on its castling destination square.

3. Each player may castle at most one time per game.

4. Castling is permanently illegal for any king or rook that was moved in an earlier ply. Rooks created by pawn promotion can never castle (they are considered to have moved from their setup square).

5. Castling is temporarily illegal if any square from the origin square through the destination square (inclusive) of the king is occupied by any piece other than the king

or chosen rook. The same restriction applies to the origin and destination squares of the chosen rook.

6. Castling is temporarily illegal if any square from the origin square through the destination square (inclusive) of the king is a square on which the king is or would be in check. There is no analogous restriction for the chosen rook.

7. After castling, the king and chosen rook will both reside on the same row they have shared from the beginning of the game (row 1 for White, row 8 for Black).

8. Before castling, the chosen rook is closer to one edge column ('a' or 'h') than is the king. But after castling, that chosen rook must be further from that edge column than is the king.

9. After castling, the king must reside in either column 'c' or 'g', for what are called "a-side" or "h-side" castling respectively. After castling, the king and chosen rook pair must reside on either columns Kc/Rd or Kg/Rf.

Chess960 Rule Set Completeness

Rule B1: FRC rules apply by default.

Unless otherwise stated, all FRC rules apply to chess960.

Rule B2: Touch move rules for castling.

1. To castle, either the king, chosen rook, or both must make a maneuver that would be illegal outside the context of castling. The only case where both pieces

must make an illegal move is when they were initially set up on each other's castling destination square.

2. Sometimes the king or rook will already be on its castling destination square before the castling ply begins: we consider it a legal maneuver for the king or rook to remain on its castling destination square during castling.

3. The touch move rule is fully in effect during castling. To avoid unpleasant issues, players are encouraged to always begin the castling ply by making an illegal movement of the king or rook. There are several plausible ways of doing this. After any of these illegal movements, the player may promptly proceed to place both his king and rook on their castling destination squares without further worry for the details of touch move rules.

4. *Simplest option:* Always begin by moving the king off the board, to just behind its castling destination square. Any move off the board is obviously illegal. Then position the rook. Finish by positioning the king.

5. *King takes rook option:* Begin by using your king to displace your rook. This is always illegal, of course. Then position the rook. Finish by repositioning the king. This maps to a logical way raw coordinate notation denotes castling in chess960 (as explained in the FEN chapter).

6. *Elegant option:* Of your king or rook, move first which ever piece must make an otherwise illegal move. Implicitly, this is what chess1 players have always done.

7. *Verbal option:* When in doubt about the touch move rules for castling, a player can simply announce

"castling" before moving the two pieces. This is similar to a player announcing "adjust" when he refines a piece to the center of its square.

Rule B3: Setup notation.

1. Chess960 requires an algebraic notation. No form of old descriptive notation is acceptable.

2. Proper score sheet notation requires that the initial setup be recorded before the game starts. This should always include the setup string format, such as RNBQ-KBNR for the traditional setup, representing columns a-h.

3. A numeric setup identification number from an approved system may be added (see R# and S#). It is optional, but inclusion is recommended if the number is known.

Rule B3.1: Optional adjustments to random setup selection.

1. In the present era where chess1 dominates the chess world, chess960 Tournament Directors have the option of pre-announcing that the chess1 setup R#362 is barred and will not be used in the unlikely event that it is the randomly chosen setup. If necessary, an additional random generation can be made to choose another setup. The reciprocal setup of the chess1 setup may also be barred, namely R#862 RNBK-QBNR.

2. Tournament Directors have the option of either using the same randomly chosen setup for all games within one round, or of randomly assigning a different setup to each individual game within each round.

3. Tournament Directors have the option of rerunning the random setup selection process any time a later round chooses a setup already used in an earlier round, though this is discouraged.

4. Tournament Directors are encouraged to delay both the random generation and the announcement of the setup until shortly before the setup is needed, perhaps on the scale of 5-15 minutes beforehand.

5. For correspondence tournaments, or for unusual real time tournaments, Tournament Directors have the option of announcing the chess960 initial setup far in advance, such as a year in advance. For general chess960 play this is strongly discouraged.

Rule B3.2: Random setup selection, with dice.

Chess960 setups should be randomly chosen by means that are simple, that use a minimum of technology, and that are transparent to any observer. Unnecessary usage of any electronic random generation device is discouraged. Dice can be a good mechanism. However, not all algorithms for using dice give each legal setup an equal chance of being selected.

Through his editing of Wikipedia.org (search for chess960), David A. Wheeler reports that Hans L. Bodlaender was the first to suggest what I call the BNQ method (mnemonically "Bobby Never Quit"). I call it BNQ because this method places the pieces in the sequence of bishops – knights – queen. At the end of the BNQ placements, the king and two rooks automatically place themselves.

The BNQ method is very convenient. A single standard six sided die, or d6, is sufficient. Having additional dice, such as a d4 of d12, can reduce or eliminate the annoying need to occasionally re-roll. The BNQ method is unbiased, meaning it gives an equal chance to every setup.

When we speak of two or more eligible squares on row 1, we consider the first eligible square to be the one closest to the 'a' side of the board. Obviously any square already occupied is ineligible. Sometimes unoccupied squares are ineligible, such as methods which roll to place the king must avoid a1 and h1 at a minimum.

Rule B3.2.1: Bodlaender's BNQ method.

1. Place the two (White) bishops. The board's first square is a1, a1 is a dark shade square, so we first place the dark square bishop.

2. There are four eligible squares, namely the four dark squares. Roll the d6 die until a number 1-4 occurs (5-6 require re-rolling). For a 1, place the bishop on the first eligible square a1, for a 2, place the bishop on the second eligible square c1, and so on.

3. Roll again to place the light square bishop. Rolling a 1 indicates square b1, a 2 indicates d1, and so on.

4. Place the two knights. The first knight has 6 eligible squares, so no re-rolling will be needed for it.

5. Place the queen. Re-roll until a 1-4 occurs.

6. On the 3 empty squares that remain, place the king and two rooks so the king is between the rooks.

BNQ is not the only valid sequence, but it is one of the simplest to calculate the combinations for, B*B*N*N*Q*RKR:

$$4 * 4 * 6 * 5 * 4 * 1 = 1920$$

Since the two knights are indistinguishable from each other, we divide 1920/2=960.

B3.2.1.1 Risk of Bias: Caution is advised when trying sequences different from BNQ. For example, we can imagine a method NQB. This might seem an equivalent method, since it will always be possible to place both bishops. Yet if BNQ and NQB were each run 960,000 times, we would see an even distribution in only the BNQ results. The NQB method would be biased against some setups.

We can see the BNQ and NQB methods are different by examining the chance each gives to having the two knights start on the same shade of square. A brute force tally from all 960 setups shows there is a 40% chance the two knights will start on the same shade. When the knights are placed during the BNQ method, there remain three light and three dark squares open, and all are eligible. After one knight is placed, it is easy to see there is a $2/5 = 40.0\%$ chance the second knight will be placed on the same shade as the first knight. This matches the 40% figure from the direct tally. In contrast, the NQB method has a $3/7 = 42.9\%$ chance the second knight will be placed on the same shade. Worded informally, the underlying problem with the NQB sequence is that the number of valid combinations the two bishops can add is reduced by the prior placements. Bishops are naturally rather restricted, so they are influenced excessively by any prior placements.

Piece per Square Probabilities: David G. Leonard, A.S.A., has provided the piece per square probabilities table shown below. All unbiased placement methods will match those probabilities. The data in this table also illuminate particular trends that will emerge over many chess960 games. For instance, the K row shows the king will be placed in a central column frequently, over 42% of the time. The two R rows for the 'a' and 'h' wing rooks show each will often be setup on an edge column. Thus the traditional chess1 RKR placement will be tied for the single most common RKR placement in chess960.

Chess960 Piece per Square % Probabilities

Piece	Column Letter								
	a	b	c	d	e	f	g	h	
R-a	37.5	26.3	18.1	10.6	5.6	1.9	0	0	100
N-a	12.5	12.5	12.5	12.5	12.5	12.5	12.5	12.5	100
B-dark	25.0	0	25.0	0	25.0	0	25.0	0	100
Q	12.5	12.5	12.5	12.5	12.5	12.5	12.5	12.5	100
K	0	11.3	17.5	21.3	21.3	17.5	11.3	0	100
B-light	0	25.0	0	25.0	0	25.0	0	25.0	100
N-h	12.5	12.5	12.5	12.5	12.5	12.5	12.5	12.5	100
R-h	0	0	1.9	5.6	10.6	18.1	26.3	37.5	100
	100	100	100	100	100	100	100	100	

Rule B3.2.2: D10 Id chart reference method.

A d10 die can be rolled three times to generate a single three digit number. It helps us that a d10 has sides numbered 0-9, not 1-10. If our three rolls are 0 & 6 & 8, then our three digit number is 068 (keep leading zeros).

That number can be combined with the R# charts presented later in this book, to cross-reference one exact piece setup string. The R# charts tell us that 068 is setup QNBB-RKRN (Q on a1).

Between 000-999 there are 40 unused Id numbers. Re-rolling will be necessary if any of those 40 arise. Any non-mathematician can easily see this method gives every setup an equal chance of being chosen. This method is transparent, except that the chart must be trusted.

Rule B3.3: No dice available.
Rule B3.3.1: No dice available, coin only situation.

In the unfortunate case that no die is available, any randomizing binary device can be used for informal play. A normal coin is the typical example. The method is to flip the coin twice. The small chart below shows how the coin flips combine to generate a number 1-4.

A simpler way is to flip two coins of different denominations, like a dime and a nickel. Treat the higher denomination coin as the first coin flip.

First Coin Flip		Second Coin Flip		Generated Number
HEAD	+	HEAD	=	1
HEAD	+	tail	=	2
tail	+	HEAD	=	3
tail	+	tail	=	4

Place the pieces in the following BKRQ sequence. Robert H. Enders described this method in *Chess Life* 2004/03. It is designed to never have more than four eligible squares at any step. Sometimes there may be only three eligible squares, so re-flipping may be necessary. Flip only one coin when there are only two eligible squares (head=1, tail=2). This BKRQ method is unbiased.

1. Bishops, dark square first.

2. King. The two unoccupied squares closest to their respective edges are ineligible. We must leave them empty to ensure the king can be between the two rooks.

3. The rook on the 'a' side of the king. Then the 'h' side rook.

4. Queen. One of three remaining open squares.

5. Knights. Simply fill the two open squares.

Rule B3.3.2: No dice, no coin, use pieces as coins.

1. **Pieces:** To mimic two coins, have four pieces in a bag: two opposite color pawns plus two opposite color queens. The person blindly draws one of each type piece, queen and pawn (his hand can feel the difference). The pawns would be equivalent to the first coin flip, the queens to the second. Treat White as a head, and Black as a tail.

Rule B3.4: No using notes after setup announced.

In chess1 and chess960, it is of course illegal for any player to reference any written matter during his game, such as chess books or any other media. In chess960 this same prohibition begins once the particular setup is announced.

4
Setup Id Numbers

Any chess960 setup can be notated by a short piece setup string such as RNBQ-KBNR. Chess computer programs use a similar kind of string in PGN files (see the chapter on FEN). Computers need no other setup Id format. While this setup string notation is handy for people too, there are times when this format is unwieldy for people, such as in conversation. To help chess players (not computers), the need was recognized for a corresponding three digit numeric identifier for setups.

There have been several setup Id systems invented. Fernand Joseph published one on the web in 2003/12 (see evonet.be/~marcsmet/ebbs/download/ FRC_960Pos.pdf), based on an iterative computer algorithm. His presentation of a piece string for all 960 setups can be a handy way to manually confirm the probabilities of various attributes occurring when randomly selecting a setup. It is a misleading coincidence that Joseph's method assigns 518 the chess1 setup, just as does the different S# system described below. Joseph's system divides the 960 setups into two reciprocal halves, but not in as useful a manner as does the R# system described below. The web site ChessGames.com uses a system built on the base 5 numbering system, which is also heavily dependent on an iterative computer program. Both of these systems are interesting or handy in their own way, but I believe there are even better systems available.

This book will use and recommend the adoption of what I call the "R#" (R number) system. The 'R' stands for 'reciprocal-pair' for reasons that will be explained. In Mainz, the Chess Tigers have a web page provided by Reinhard Scharnagl, which describes Scharnagl's proposed Id system. The system seems unnamed, so I call it "S#", where 'S' stands for Scharnagl, the name of its primary inventor. For the chess1 setup the Ids are R#362 or S#518. The corresponding piece setup string is RNBQ-KBNR.

Due to the great work by the Chess Tigers, as of 2005, a fast growing number of chess playing programs are now chess960 capable, including Fritz9, Hiarcs10, Shredder, and the Mainz 2005 computer chess960 champion Spike. ChessMaster, its 10th edition released in 2005, is still unable to play chess960.

Some of these chess programs have implemented numeric Id systems for the chess960 setups. Several have adopted the S# system. Unfortunately they do not name their system, as if there were only one system so far invented. At this very early stage of chess960, it is too early to close the door on innovation and improvement, or to assume the long term dominance of one specific system. The spirit of chess960 is all about change for improvement. I will suggest the R# system be implemented in the chess playing programs of the world. A competition of ideas is a healthy way to produce the best system.

The chess playing program Fritz9 uses its own setup Id system, which I call F#. At this writing I have not yet been able to perceive the advantage the F# system inventors presumably see their system having over the more well known S#. Of those two, the S# seems easier to use (as explained below). So I will not go into the full formulaic details of the F# system.

I strongly believe there should be absolutely no copyright claims poised to hinder the republication of anything having to do with any chess960 setup Id system being proposed for world-wide adoption. That is why in the front of this book I have used my copyrights to grant broad permissions pertaining to the R# system.

The ideal numeric Id system will achieve all of the following goals.

Major Goals:

(A) Enable people to easily convert from the Id number to its corresponding setup string. Unfortunately people will likely need charts to make this practical.

(B) Enable people to easily convert from the setup string to its corresponding Id number.

(C) Have the charts needed for goals A & B be dually sorted for easy conversion in both directions.

(D) Given an Id, enable people to very easily determine the Id for its reciprocal setup. For instance, one reciprocal-pair of setups is NNBB-RKRQ & QRKR-BBNN. These are R#085 & R#585 respectively. This handy feature helps when your friend tells you he just finished a game using R#085, and you remember that last week you played using R#585 (the difference always being an easy round 500).

Minor Goals:

(E) Require the fewest lines of computer programming language source code possible. This is not a major goal because computers should serve people, not the reverse. Also, even systems not designed for maximum algorithmic or mathematic elegance present no difficulties for programming.

(F) Encode for whether the queen or king was closer to the 'a' column.

In brief, the R# system achieves goals A+B+C+D+F, while the S# system achieves goals A+B+C+E. This explains my reasons for believing the R# is an excellent setup Id system. The F# system achieves only A+E.

Rule B4: Id numbers for setups.

Rule B4.1: R# numeric Id system for setups.

A couple pages below there are two tables, one large and one small. We can call the large table the "R# Relative Positions" tables, or Rpt. We can call the small table the "Bishop" table, or Bt. Each table is dually sorted, both numerically and by piece icon position features. The numeric sorting chosen favors R# over S#. Either table could be re-sorted to better favor S# numbers over R# numbers.

What follows next is an example of using the Rpt and Bt tables in the R# system. The technique would be nearly the same for using the S# system, except numeric columns in Bt labeled S# would be used instead of those labeled R#.

R# Conversion from Id to setup string: Say you are given Id R#141.

1. In the R# Relative Positions table (Rpt), find the highest number that does not exceed 141. This means the Rpt row numbered 128 (QNRNKR), Rpt=128.

2. In the Rpt row, note whether the K or Q is closer to column 'a'. In this case the Q is the more 'a' side of the two royal pieces (always true for R# when Rpt < 500). This datum will determine which column we use in the Bt table.

3. Subtract the Rpt value from the input R# number. In this case 141-128=13. This difference helps determine the relevant row in the Bt table (.B..B...), Bt=13.

4. Next we will reference the Bt table, focusing on the column labeled R#_QK (not R#_KQ). We will use this Bt column because in our earlier Rpt row we noted the Q is more 'a' side than is the Q. Under Bt column R#_QK, find the row labeled 13, because above we calculated Bt=13. This Bt row gives the required exact positions of the two bishops, filling two of the eight squares in chess board row 1 (in this case b1 and e1).

5. Fill in the remaining six squares as guided by the sequence in the Rpt table row.

6. The result means R#141 is QBNR-BNKR.

R# Conversion from setup string to Id: Say you are given RKNB-RNBQ (the reciprocal of R#141).

1. Think of the input setup string without the bishops. Envision this string as RKN.-RN.Q (dots being placeholders for irrelevant bishops). Note the K is the first royal piece (is closer to column 'a' than is the Q).

2. In this case the K occurs first, so the Rpt table row will be in the second half.

3. The piece icons in the Rpt table are also sorted, in two levels. (a) The primary sorting is by the position of the queen. In this case the queen is in the sixth or right-most relative position. (b) The secondary sorting is by the quantity of pieces that reside between the two royal pieces (again, bishops excluded). In this case three pieces are set up between the K and Q (NRN).

4. Leverage the icon sorting to easily find the matching Rpt row piece string for the input string. Once matched, note the row number under column R#, in this case Rpt=628.

5. Find the Bt table row that matches the setup string. In our input piece string RKNB-RNBQ the bishops are in

columns 'd' and 'g'. This matches the bottom row in the Bt table. Here we use the Bt=13 under the R#_KQ column (the K is more 'a' side than the Q).

6. Add Rpt + Bt = R#. In this case 628 + 13 = R#641.

R# Special considerations:

Reciprocal Id: The R# system purposely skips numbers in the range 480-499. This means the R# number range is 0-979. The S# system skips no numbers and its range is 0-959. The R# system skips the 480-499 range so that the two setups in each reciprocal-pair can have their R# Ids differ by exactly 500, a round number easy for people to add and subtract. This is why R#980 is not a valid equivalent of R#000, even informally.

The chess1 setup has Ids R#362 and S#518. We immediately know that the reciprocal Id for R#362 must be R#862, but we have no immediate way of knowing that the reciprocal of S#518 is S#534.

Three digits: It is recommended that all three digits always be used. Correct is R#002, incorrect is R#2.

Next are the Rpt tables for the S# and R# Id systems, followed by the one Bt table that serves both. For a system like R#, these tables can be used to do the following:

- Convert from an R# value to the piece string.
- Convert from a piece string to the R#.

- Extra tables are included, each sorted to optimize Id conversions between systems in different directions.

S# Relative Positions Table (Rpt), a-h

S#	a – h	S#	a – h
000	♛ ♘ ♘ ♖ ♔ ♖	480	♛ ♖ ♘ ♔ ♘ ♖
016	♘ ♛ ♘ ♖ ♔ ♖	496	♖ ♛ ♘ ♔ ♘ ♖
032	♘ ♘ ♛ ♖ ♔ ♖	512	♖ ♘ ♛ ♔ ♘ ♖
048	♘ ♘ ♖ ♛ ♔ ♖	528	♖ ♘ ♔ ♛ ♘ ♖
064	♘ ♘ ♖ ♔ ♛ ♖	544	♖ ♘ ♔ ♘ ♛ ♖
080	♘ ♘ ♖ ♔ ♖ ♛	560	♖ ♘ ♔ ♘ ♖ ♛
096	♛ ♘ ♖ ♘ ♔ ♖	576	♛ ♖ ♘ ♔ ♖ ♘
112	♘ ♛ ♖ ♘ ♔ ♖	592	♖ ♛ ♘ ♔ ♖ ♘
128	♘ ♖ ♛ ♘ ♔ ♖	608	♖ ♘ ♛ ♔ ♖ ♘
144	♘ ♖ ♘ ♛ ♔ ♖	624	♖ ♘ ♔ ♛ ♖ ♘
160	♘ ♖ ♘ ♔ ♛ ♖	640	♖ ♘ ♔ ♖ ♛ ♘
176	♘ ♖ ♘ ♔ ♖ ♛	656	♖ ♘ ♔ ♖ ♘ ♛
192	♛ ♘ ♖ ♖ ♔ ♘	672	♛ ♖ ♖ ♔ ♘ ♘
208	♘ ♛ ♖ ♖ ♔ ♘	688	♖ ♛ ♖ ♔ ♘ ♘
224	♘ ♖ ♛ ♖ ♔ ♘	704	♖ ♖ ♛ ♔ ♘ ♘
240	♘ ♖ ♖ ♛ ♔ ♘	720	♖ ♖ ♔ ♛ ♘ ♘
256	♘ ♖ ♖ ♔ ♛ ♘	736	♖ ♖ ♔ ♘ ♛ ♘
272	♘ ♖ ♖ ♔ ♘ ♛	752	♖ ♖ ♔ ♘ ♘ ♛
288	♛ ♘ ♖ ♔ ♖ ♘	768	♛ ♖ ♔ ♘ ♖ ♘
304	♘ ♛ ♖ ♔ ♖ ♘	784	♖ ♛ ♔ ♘ ♖ ♘
320	♘ ♖ ♛ ♔ ♖ ♘	800	♖ ♔ ♛ ♘ ♖ ♘
336	♘ ♖ ♔ ♛ ♖ ♘	816	♖ ♔ ♘ ♛ ♖ ♘
352	♘ ♖ ♔ ♖ ♛ ♘	832	♖ ♔ ♘ ♖ ♛ ♘
368	♘ ♖ ♔ ♖ ♘ ♛	848	♖ ♔ ♘ ♖ ♘ ♛
384	♛ ♖ ♘ ♘ ♔ ♖	864	♛ ♖ ♔ ♖ ♘ ♘
400	♖ ♛ ♘ ♘ ♔ ♖	880	♖ ♛ ♔ ♖ ♘ ♘
416	♖ ♘ ♛ ♘ ♔ ♖	896	♖ ♔ ♛ ♖ ♘ ♘
432	♖ ♘ ♘ ♛ ♔ ♖	912	♖ ♔ ♖ ♛ ♘ ♘
448	♖ ♘ ♘ ♔ ♛ ♖	928	♖ ♔ ♖ ♘ ♛ ♘
464	♖ ♘ ♘ ♔ ♖ ♛	944	♖ ♔ ♖ ♘ ♘ ♛

R# Relative Positions Table (Rpt), a-h

R# ♛♔	a – h					
000	♛	♖	♔	♘	♘	♖
016	♛	♖	♔	♘	♖	♘
032	♛	♖	♔	♖	♘	♘
048	♛	♘	♖	♔	♘	♖
064	♛	♘	♖	♔	♖	♘
080	♛	♖	♘	♔	♘	♖
096	♛	♖	♘	♔	♖	♘
112	♛	♘	♘	♔	♖	♖
128	♛	♘	♖	♔	♘	♖
144	♛	♖	♘	♘	♔	♖
160	♖	♛	♔	♘	♘	♖
176	♖	♛	♔	♘	♖	♘
192	♖	♛	♔	♖	♘	♘
208	♘	♛	♖	♔	♘	♖
224	♘	♛	♖	♔	♖	♘
240	♖	♛	♘	♔	♘	♖
256	♖	♛	♘	♔	♖	♘
272	♘	♛	♘	♖	♔	♖
288	♘	♛	♖	♘	♔	♖
304	♖	♛	♘	♘	♔	♖
320	♘	♖	♛	♔	♘	♖
336	♘	♖	♛	♔	♖	♘
352	♖	♘	♛	♔	♘	♖
368	♖	♘	♛	♔	♖	♘
384	♘	♘	♛	♖	♔	♖
400	♘	♖	♛	♘	♔	♖
416	♖	♘	♛	♘	♔	♖
432	♘	♘	♖	♛	♔	♖
448	♘	♖	♘	♛	♔	♖
464	♖	♘	♘	♛	♔	♖

R# ♚♕	a – h					
500	♖	♘	♘	♚	♖	♕
516	♘	♖	♘	♚	♖	♕
532	♘	♘	♖	♚	♖	♕
548	♖	♘	♚	♖	♘	♕
564	♘	♖	♚	♖	♘	♕
580	♖	♘	♚	♘	♖	♕
596	♘	♖	♚	♘	♖	♕
612	♖	♚	♖	♘	♘	♕
628	♖	♚	♘	♖	♘	♕
644	♖	♚	♘	♘	♖	♕
660	♖	♘	♘	♚	♕	♖
676	♘	♖	♘	♚	♕	♖
692	♘	♘	♖	♚	♕	♖
708	♖	♘	♚	♖	♕	♘
724	♘	♖	♚	♖	♕	♘
740	♖	♘	♚	♘	♕	♖
756	♘	♖	♚	♘	♕	♖
772	♖	♚	♖	♘	♕	♘
788	♖	♚	♘	♖	♕	♘
804	♖	♚	♘	♘	♕	♖
820	♖	♘	♚	♕	♖	♘
836	♘	♖	♚	♕	♖	♘
852	♖	♘	♚	♕	♘	♖
868	♘	♖	♚	♕	♘	♖
884	♖	♚	♖	♕	♘	♘
900	♖	♚	♘	♕	♖	♘
916	♖	♚	♘	♕	♘	♖
932	♖	♚	♕	♖	♘	♘
948	♖	♚	♕	♘	♖	♘
964	♖	♚	♕	♘	♘	♖

Bishop Table (Bt)

R# <500 ♛♚	a	b	c	d	e	f	g	h	R# >=500 ♚♛	S#, F#
00	♗			♗					01	01
01				♗			♗		00	11
02	♗	♗							07	00
03		♗	♗						06	04
04			♗	♗					05	05
05				♗	♗				04	10
06					♗	♗			03	14
07						♗	♗		02	15
08	♗							♗	08	03
09		♗					♗		09	12
10			♗			♗			10	06
11				♗	♗				11	09
12	♗					♗			14	02
13		♗			♗				15	08
14			♗					♗	12	07
15				♗			♗		13	13
♛♚ <500 R#		Placement of the two White Bishops.				♚♛ >=500 R#				S#, F#

Root Cross-Reference Tables: S# & R#

S#	R#	S#	R#	S#	R#	S#	R#
000	112	240	868	480	080	720	916
016	272	256	756	496	240	736	804
032	384	272	596	512	352	752	644
048	432	288	064	528	852	768	016
064	692	304	224	544	740	784	176
080	532	320	336	560	580	800	948
096	128	336	836	576	096	816	900
112	288	352	724	592	256	832	788
128	400	368	564	608	368	848	628
144	448	384	144	624	820	864	032
160	676	400	304	640	708	880	192
176	516	416	416	656	548	896	932
192	048	432	464	672	000	912	884
208	208	448	660	688	160	928	772
224	320	464	500	704	964	944	612

(Bt)

S#, F#	R#	
	QK	KQ
00	02	07
01	00	01
02	12	14
03	08	08
04	03	06
05	04	05
06	10	10
07	14	12
08	13	15
09	11	11
10	05	04
11	01	00
12	09	09
13	15	13
14	06	03
15	07	02

R#	S#	R#	S#	R#	S#	R#	S#
000	672	240	496	500	464	740	544
016	768	256	592	516	176	756	256
032	864	272	016	532	080	772	928
048	192	288	112	548	656	788	832
064	288	304	400	564	368	804	736
080	480	320	224	580	560	820	624
096	576	336	320	596	272	836	336
112	000	352	512	612	944	852	528
128	096	368	608	628	848	868	240
144	384	384	032	644	752	884	912
160	688	400	128	660	448	900	816
176	784	416	416	676	160	916	720
192	880	432	048	692	064	932	896
208	208	448	144	708	640	948	800
224	304	464	432	724	352	964	704

Root Cross-Reference Tables: F# & R#

R# QK	F#	R#	F#	R# KQ	F#	R#	F#
000	192	240	400	500	800	740	576
016	208	256	416	516	736	756	512
032	224	272	016	532	720	772	928
048	112	288	032	548	832	788	896
064	128	304	384	564	768	804	624
080	160	320	288	580	816	820	608
096	176	336	304	596	752	836	544
112	080	352	352	612	912	852	592
128	096	368	368	628	880	868	528
144	144	384	000	644	864	884	944
160	432	400	272	660	560	900	656
176	448	416	336	676	496	916	640
192	464	432	240	692	480	932	704
208	048	448	256	708	848	948	688
224	064	464	320	724	784	964	672

F# QK	R#	F#	R#	F# KQ	R#	F#	R#
000	384	240	432	480	692	720	532
016	272	256	448	496	676	736	516
032	288	272	400	512	756	752	596
048	208	288	320	528	868	768	564
064	224	304	336	544	836	784	724
080	112	320	464	560	660	800	500
096	128	336	416	576	740	816	580
112	048	352	352	592	852	832	548
128	064	368	368	608	820	848	708
144	144	384	304	624	804	864	644
160	080	400	240	640	916	880	628
176	096	416	256	656	900	896	788
192	000	432	160	672	964	912	612
208	016	448	256	688	948	928	772
224	032	464	320	704	932	944	884

F# Relative Positions Table (Rpt), a-h

F#	a - h	F#	a - h
000	♞♞♛♜♚♜	240	♞♞♜♛♚♜
016	♞♛♞♜♚♜	256	♞♜♞♛♚♜
032	♞♛♜♞♚♜	272	♞♜♛♞♚♜
048	♞♛♜♚♞♜	288	♞♜♛♚♞♜
064	♞♛♜♚♜♞	304	♞♜♛♚♜♞
080	♛♞♞♜♚♜	320	♜♞♞♛♚♜
096	♛♞♜♞♚♜	336	♜♞♛♞♚♜
112	♛♞♜♚♞♜	352	♜♞♛♚♞♜
128	♛♞♜♚♜♞	368	♜♞♛♚♜♞
144	♛♜♞♞♚♜	384	♜♛♞♞♚♜
160	♛♜♞♚♞♜	400	♜♛♞♚♞♜
176	♛♜♞♚♜♞	416	♜♛♞♚♜♞
192	♛♜♚♞♞♜	432	♜♛♚♞♞♜
208	♛♜♚♞♜♞	448	♜♛♚♞♜♞
224	♛♜♚♜♞♞	464	♜♛♚♜♞♞

F#	a - h	F#	a - h
480	♞♞♜♚♛♜	720	♞♞♜♚♜♛
496	♞♜♞♚♛♜	736	♞♜♞♚♜♛
512	♞♜♚♞♛♜	752	♞♜♚♞♜♛
528	♞♜♚♛♞♜	768	♞♜♚♜♞♛
544	♞♜♚♛♜♞	784	♞♜♚♜♛♞
560	♜♞♞♚♛♜	800	♜♞♞♚♜♛
576	♜♞♚♞♛♜	816	♜♞♚♞♜♛
592	♜♞♚♛♞♜	832	♜♞♚♜♞♛
608	♜♞♚♛♜♞	848	♜♞♚♜♛♞
624	♜♚♞♞♛♜	864	♜♚♞♞♜♛
640	♜♚♞♛♞♜	880	♜♚♞♜♞♛
656	♜♚♞♛♜♞	896	♜♚♞♜♛♞
672	♜♚♛♞♞♜	912	♜♚♜♞♞♛
688	♜♚♛♞♜♞	928	♜♚♜♞♛♞
704	♜♚♛♜♞♞	944	♜♚♜♛♞♞

Notice 000, 240, 480, 720 differ only by Q location. Same for 016, 256, 496 etc. The knights remain put, so the queen skip over them.

Rule B4.2: S# numeric Id system for setups.

The S# system of Reinhard Scharnagl is published on the web site of the Chess Tigers, and in Scharnagl's 2004 chess960 book. The S# tables are described in this book by permission. Parts of it can also be found on Wikipedia.com.

The S# system uses the range 0-959 with no skipped numbers. There is no simple relationship between the S# Id values for the two setups in each reciprocal-pair. The S# does offer a shorter algorithm for computer programmers looking to convert between the S# Id and the piece setup string. In my judgment, making the length of the computer algorithm a higher priority than general human usability would be letting the tail wag the dog.

The S# Rpt table is used the same way as was the R# Rpt. The Bt table is also used as it was in R#, except S# is simpler because Bt contains only one S# column not two.

Rule B4.3: F# and conversions.

F# Id System: The F# system is very similar to the S# system. The F# Rpt table is used the same way for F#, as the S# Rpt table is used for S#. Both F# and S# use the same Bt table the same way. The F# algorithm ends with the addition of 1. So the F# range is 1-960, instead of 0-959 as in S#. For chess1, F#359 = S#518 (= R#362).

A customers who buys Fritz9 may find the above root conversion charts helpful when he wants to tell Fritz9 the chess960 setup he wants to play. (Late word is that ChessBase has abandonded F# in favor of S# with a patch for Fritz9.)

For different reasons, every F# value between 1-480 corresponds to some R# value between 0-479. Thus also, every F# value between 481-960 corresponds to some R# value between 500-979. However, there is no extremely easy way to determine that F#685 is the reciprocal setup to F#333, for example.

Example Conversion From R# to F#: Let us convert R#544 to the corresponding F#.

1. Find the R#-F# conversion chart.

2. Under the R# column, find the root of R#544. This will be R#532.

3. Note the F# root, as F#720, immediately to the right.

4. Use subtraction on the R# Id and root, to determine the Bt row that must be accessed next. Here 544 – 532 = 12.

5. The R#544 value is 500 or higher, so on the BT table we use the R# column marked KQ. At Bt row 12 we see the F# is 07.

6. Add the earlier F# root plus the Bt value 07. Here 720 + 7 = 727.

7. Add 1. 727 + 1 = 728. Here F#728 = R#544 (= S#087).

Rule B4.2.1: S# formulaic algorithms, using one small "KRN" chart.

The Rpt and Bt tables are somewhat large. As another option invented by Scharnagl, the S# system can calculate any given setup string from its numeric identifier, and the reverse, all with needing only one small reference chart.

Formula: input S# id, output algebraic string: Here is an example of calculating the string given numeric Id S#890 (R#197). The expected output is RQKR-BBNN.

1. 890 / 4 = 222 and r.2
Use remainder, 2, to place the light square bishop. 0=b, 1=d, 2=f, 3=h. Here 'f'.

2. 222 / 4 = 55 and r.2
Use remainder, 2, to place the dark square bishop. 0=a, 1=c, 2=e, 3=g. Here 'e'.

3. 55 / 6 = 9 and r.1
Use remainder, 1, to place the queen. In direction from column 'a' to 'h' (as always), 0=first vacant square, 1=second vacant square, ..., 5=sixth vacant square. Here 1 means 'b'.

KRN Code	Relative Placements	Corresponding Rpt section for S#
0	♞ ♞ ♜ ♚ ♜	S#000 - 095
1	♞ ♜ ♞ ♚ ♜	S#096 - 191
2	♞ ♜ ♚ ♞ ♜	S#192 - 287
3	♞ ♜ ♚ ♜ ♞	S#288 - 383
4	♜ ♞ ♞ ♚ ♜	S#384 - 479
5	♜ ♞ ♚ ♞ ♜	S#480 - 575
6	♜ ♞ ♚ ♜ ♞	S#576 - 671
7	♜ ♚ ♞ ♞ ♜	S#672 - 767
8	♜ ♚ ♞ ♜ ♞	S#768 - 863
9	♜ ♚ ♜ ♞ ♞	S#864 - 959

4. The latest truncated integer, 9, will have one of ten values in the range from 0-9 inclusive. This is called the KRN code value, derived from the pieces it encodes (king, rook,

knight). The KRN code indicates the relative placements among the remaining five pieces. We use the appropriately numbered row from the KRN table. Here our 9 means RKRNN. These five pieces fill the remaining empty squares, keeping their relative position to each other as shown in the proper KRN row.

From our input Id of S#890 we have arrived at string RQKR-BBNN.

Formula: input algebraic string, output S# Id: Here is the formula for the reverse direction.

Numeric Identifier
= 1 * Light square bishop location (b=0, d=1 etc)
+ 4 * Dark square bishop location
+ 16 * Queen location (a=0, skipping bishop squares!)
+ 96 * KRN code

Here is the usage of the above formula for our running example of S#890. Our input is RQKR-BBNN.

id
= 1 * 2 (2 is for 'f')
+ 4 * 2 (2 is for 'e')
+ 16 * 1 (1 is for queen on 'b', no bishops to skip)
+ 96 * 9 (9 is for KRN row)
= 890 S#

5

Additional Rules to Consider for Chess960

If history had not yet produced chess and we were now creating chess for the first time, I would propose a few additional rules for chess960, and probably for chess1 also. These rules are explained in this chapter.

'Whiteness': In December 2005 on Chessville.com, the Parrot lamented that the final 30 chess1 games in the Super-Final of the 58th Mens' Championship of Russia had tallied 9 wins for White and 0 wins for Black. The Parrot asked "Is chess dying of draws and 'whiteness'?". Months earlier I had written this chapter to address these exact concerns.

Proposed Chess960 Rule Set Differences From FRC

Rule C1: Fair First Move (FFM) rule.

By virtue of his unfettered first move, in legacy chess White has an unfair advantage (there is no other kind). Black wins only 3 games for every 4 White wins. The FFM rule would eliminate this unsporting aspect from chess. The game of Twixt uses the FFM rule. By principle, this FFM rule may remind us of the fair minded mother who tells her son to cut a cupcake in half then lets her daughter choose whichever half she prefers.

1. The game always begins with White making the first ply, such as perhaps 1. h23.

2. Black has two options for his first ply. One option Black has is to make a normal reply of his own choosing, such as 1... e75.

   Alternatively Black has the option of undoing White's first ply and "adopting" the mirror move for himself. In this example Black would first physically move White's Ph3 back to h2. Black would then immediately be required to move h76 (h76 being the Black mirror of White's h23).

3. Black has this adoption option only on his first ply, and White never has it. After Black completes his first ply, the jurisdiction of this FFM rule is ended. All subsequent plies proceed as normal.

4. White's first physical move will always be considered as White's first ply, regardless of whether Black chooses to adopt White's first ply. This means White's first move counts as a ply toward meeting the time controls even if Black chooses to adopt White's first move.

5. This also means score sheet numberings and clock move counters need no adjustment based on Black's FFM decision. We need only introduce the concept of a retroactive null move for White in some games.

6. If Black touches any of his own movable pieces before returning White's piece to its initial square, then Black loses the option of adopting White's first ply. If Black touches the moved White piece before touching any

movable Black piece, then Black must adopt White's first ply.

7. Score sheets will need to notate whether Black chose to adopt White's first ply. If Black decides not to adopt, this will be passively notated by the simple absence of any special notation.

If Black does decide to adopt White's first ply, the score sheet box for White's first ply will be notated to indicate this adoption. White's first ply would be prefixed by adding two down-left slashes. The slashes notate that Black nullified and took White's first ply. Notation examples follow:

1. //a23   a76
1. //Ng1f3   Ng8f6

8. This FFM rule gives Tournament Directors more flexibility in their traditional responsibility of carefully assigning White and Black an even number of times to each player. Sometimes a Tournament Director is compelled to assign a particular player to be Black three games in a rows. Under the FFM rule this no longer is a problem for the player, making tournaments easier to run. Standard four player "quad" tournaments no longer need to be unfair to those half of the players forced to have Black more often than White.

9. Where the FFM rule is used, the R# value remains unchanged regardless of whether Black exercises his first-ply option. The piece setup string also remains unchanged. Logically the game is unchanged. A game using R#412 does not become a reciprocal game of R#912 by Black adopting White's first ply. Instead, the colors and algebraic row numbers become transposed to a

visually different but logically equivalent setup. The relationships between the pieces and the primary castling squares on columns 'c' and 'g' are not changed.

Unfortunately this does mean that it could be laborious to compare two games that use the same R# setup when in exactly one of those games the Black player adopted White's first ply. A transposition of notated moves to the White perspective would be needed to make comparison plausible. Software could do this transposition.

Rule C2: Draw Offer Duration 2 (DOD2) rule.

Most of the discussions about the draw problem in chess are about pre-agreed draws between grandmasters. But there are other kinds of draw problems in chess.

When a middle game position is unclear or complex, both players may become fearful of losing. To avoid losing, one player may offer a draw, because there is no added risk for him to do so. The problem is that some exciting games are terminated prematurely. Even just knowing the painless draw offer option is available has a negative psychological effect during the game. It contrasts sharply with the psychological state Hernando Cortes set in his soldiers in Mexico in 1519. According to exaggerated legend, Cortes ordered his ships burned so his men would be left with a sharp mentality of fight or die: there was no longer the third possibility of returning safely to Spain.

As in any honorable sport, a chess game should continue anytime the position remains unresolved. Ideally there would be a penalty for offering a draw prematurely, yet no penalty for offering a draw in a clearly resolved position. This DOD2 rule is designed to meet those objectives. I first saw this idea in Larry Evans' column in *Chess Life*, some time around 1988-1992. The DOD2 rule applies equally well to chess960 and to chess1.

1. The rules about draw offers are the same in chess960 as they are in chess1, except as noted below.

2. A draw offer expires after the receiving player completes his second subsequent ply, not yet after he completes his first subsequent ply.

3. This DOD2 rule is not meant to interfere with the special case of a Tournament Director declaring a late endgame position to be a known theoretical draw.

Under DOD2, a player offering a draw in a genuinely resolved position brings himself no added risk in the practical sense. But it would be risky or even foolish for player AA to offer a draw prematurely in a complex middle game position. It would be giving his opponent BB a safe way to make a challenging but speculative move. Player AA would be forced to make a correct reply. After seeing AA's move, BB could accept the draw if he believes AA made a strong reply or has obtained the advantage. If AA failed to find the necessary reply, BB could reject the draw offer (by ignoring it) and proceed with improved winning chances.

Adopting the DOD2 rule would enable us to remove awkward language from the chess rule book that vaguely makes it illegal to make too many draw offers to your opponent.

Deep Junior 2003 and Kasparov: In New York in 2003 a televised chess match was held between then former WCC Garry Kasparov and a personal computer running the chess program Deep Junior. The public image of chess suffered on the day of the sixth and final game. There arose an interesting and materially unbalanced position created by an exchange sacrifice by Kasparov. Deep Junior's human operator offered a draw and Kasparov accepted. This premature ending was greeted with some outrage, and it became the biggest news story of the match. Both sides were motivated by fear and their desire to not lose the overall match, which ended in a tie at +1-

1=4. Had the DOD2 rule been if effect when Kasparov played Deep Junior in New York in 2003, the Deep Junior operator probably would not have dared to extend this infamous draw offer to Kasparov.

Rule C3: Opposite Wing Castling (OWC) rule reasoning.

This is the only on-the-board rule change I am advocating for chess960. This rule change is somewhat like a return to the castling rule that was used in some countries at least as late as 1777, according to what Andre Philidor wrote in the 1777 edition of his book *Analysis of the Game of Chess* (see Bill Wall's web pages at geocities.com/siliconvalley/lab/7378/, such as philidor.htm).

In chess1 there is an awful problem with the high frequency of draws. Castling to the same wing leads to a higher percentage of draws than does opposite wing castling. According to a Mega Database 2004 search, about 34% of same wing castling games end in a draw, whereas only 24% of opposite wing castling games end in a draw. So it is unfortunate that the legacy chess rule set leads in most games to same wing castling. Of all games where both players castled, only 8% of those games had castling to opposite wings.

There are two features of the legacy chess rule set that contribute to the particular castling rates we see. First, in the chess1 setup more back row pieces must be developed before 'a' wing castling can occur than before 'h' wing. Second, 'a' wing castling leaves the king too far from a protective corner compared to what 'h' wing castling provides. Around the year 1475 the chess lords must have felt it would be unseemly for castling to take the king more than two squares away. They could not foresee the draw problem their assessment would help create.

Early indications are that FRC suffers from this same problem of too much same wing castling. I scanned the subset of tournament data available on the Mainz website, but even that data is rather sparse in absolute terms. Though probably not statistically significant, it looks like 'h' wing castling is a little more popular than is 'a' wing in chess960. If this proves out as a reliable preference for 'h' wing castling over 'a' wing, we would probably conclude players do not like their castled king being far from the protective corner.

Bobby Fischer wanted to make FRC as close to chess1 as possible so as to aid in the adoption of FRC. It would not have worked for Fischer to say "In FRC the castling king moves two squares in either direction, just as it does in chess1" (imagine such a rule in cases where the king starts on b1 or g1). So Fischer chose to make the king and chosen rook destination squares the same in FRC as they are in chess1. This is simple and easy to explain. The problem is that the asymmetry between these two king destination squares is illogical in FRC.

Would the rate of opposite wing castling have been higher in FRC if the castling destination asymmetry had been eliminated? And would the draw rate have thus been reduced? Being realistic, just eliminating the castling asymmetry would do only slightly more than nothing toward alleviating the draw problem.

Fischer did a good job designing the FRC castling rule. However, part of me feels it squanders an exceedingly rare opportunity to make substantial progress against the draw problem. I believe there is a way we could tweak the chess960 castling rule to increase opposite wing castling. This is why I am suggesting for chess960 the OWC rule explained below.

Rule C3.1: Opposite Wing Castling (OWC) rule.

1. The castling rules of FRC apply except where modified below.

2. The 'a' wing is said to consist of columns a,b,c. The 'h' wing consists of columns f,g,h. The central area between the two wings is columns d,e.

3. When either player completes the first castling move of the game, we call him the first player and his opponent the second player.

4. The first player has the standard right to castle to column 'c' for 'a' wing castling, and to column 'g' for 'h' wing castling.

5. The second player to castle will castle to either the same or opposite wing as the first player. If the second player castles to the same wing, then his king must castle to the same column the first king castled to.

   But if the second player castles to the opposite wing, his king can choose as its destination any of the three columns on that opposite wing.

   For example, if the first player castles to the 'h' wing thus putting his king on column 'g', the second player could castle to the 'a' wing and choose for his king any column among a,b,c.

   This means the second player gains extra choices for opposite wing castling, in addition to retaining the normal castling option for same wing castling.

6. No king can ever castle to the center columns d,e.

7. The castling rook will always end on a square immediately adjacent to the king. For example, if the king castles to column 'b', then the 'a' wing rook ends on column 'c'.

Rule C3.2: Flexible Castling notation to Support OWC.

The notation for castling used in both chess1 and FRC is either O-O or O-O-O. This format is not ideal for chess960, nor is it flexible enough to support potentials like OWC. The castling move should be notated in a complete and reversible form. For example, the CRAN Kf1b/Rac would be ideal. Also good would be the more verbose Kf1-b1/Ra1-c1. If capital letter 'O' sequences are used to notate castling in chess960, O-O always means 'h' wing and O-O-O always means 'a' wing. However, neither any longer correlates with the informal concepts of castling long versus short as they are updated by chess960.

More About the Draw Problem

In my judgment the chess1 problem of excessive draws is harmful to the public image of chess. We all know how deflating it is to read that yesterday's WCC game was yet another draw. The big question about each game of a WCC title match is not who will win but whether it will be yet another draw. We know this is an unsporting image for chess, and it drains the excitement from what should be a climactic event. It makes little difference to the public whether the draw was a hard fought game or another game that retraced well worn paths through ply 48. Even chess authors rarely publish draws. In *Understanding Chess Move By Move*, John Nunn saw fit to include 0 draws among his chosen 30 games, and we would be surprised had he done otherwise.

Chess960 along with the OWC rule, is an extremely rare opportunity to reduce the draw problem. We in the chess world cannot complain about the lack of sponsorship money for chess when draws continues to dominate our sport. Why should anyone sponsor a parade of draws? In 2004 even I had a hard time getting excited each morning reading that Kramnik and Leko had yet another draw: 10 of 14 games were drawn. The previous title match between Kasparov and Kramnik was even worse: 13 of 15 games were drawn. (By the way, no WCC title match should end when the trailing player has won the latest game.)

In theory, must any two-player digital sport necessarily end in a draw if both players play error free? There are a limited number of design mechanisms available to avoid a draw every time the game is played. Below is a list of the possible mechanisms I see for reducing the draw problem in board games like chess: Complexity, Unfair Advantage, Disassociation, Luck, and Asymmetry. Each of these mechanisms is discussed in the context of chess960 rule proposals.

1. **Complexity:** Tic-Tac-Toe is an example of a game that suffers from far too little complexity. Even Garry Kasparov would never beat me in tic-tac-toe. In contrast, highly complex games rarely end in a draw. Shogi (loosely called Japanese chess) is much more complex than chess. One reason is that shogi pieces can return to the board after they have been taken. As a result, even the best Shogi players make several mistakes in each game. These mistakes create opportunities for the opponent, and eventually someone wins. The complexity level of chess1 is somewhere between tic-tac-toe and shogi.

   Blitz chess is effectively more complex than regular time control chess1 or chess960. This is why Blitz games end decisively more often than do regular time control games. Even though the Blitz version of the time control rule is drastic, time control rule changes are still just quantitative and off-the-board. Blitz is not an acceptable solution to the draw problem in chess because Blitz is too drastically different from chess1. The difficulty level in Blitz is too high for top quality play to occur. Low quality chess is not enjoyed by chess spectators who replay grandmaster games.

The complexity level of chess960 is between that of chess1 and blitz. Chess960 is more complex than chess1 because players cannot memorize the opening moves before the game. There will be a higher rate of subtle mistakes made in chess960 opening play. The as yet unanswered question is whether opponents will recognize those moves as mistakes and will know how to exploit them.

2. **Unfair Advantage:** If a board game gives one player a huge advantage over the other, the advantaged player could win often enough that draws would be rare. This would be highly unsporting. The cure would be worse than the disease. Fairness is best.

Chess1 has long suffered from an unnecessary unfairness. White accumulates about 30% more wins than does Black: roughly 4 White wins for every 3 Black wins. The significance of White's advantage has been recognized for centuries. Andre Philidor gave Philip Stamma favorable odds by giving Stamma the White pieces in every game of their match of 1747. As discussed earlier, the FFM (Fair First Move) rule proposal forces the recognition that this flaw in chess960 exists only if we let it, and that it can be solved with no harm to the game. Chess960 can adopt the FFM rule more easily than can chess1. This is because the FFM rule might narrow the range of opening moves commonly played. The range of common or sensible opening moves in chess1 is far more narrow than in chess960. Any move like 1. e24 used to open two chess960 games from different setups is really a different move. Though chess1 might be narrowed too much by FFM, there is no such risk in chess960.

3. **Disassociation:** In the game of Battleship each player populates his hidden grid with boats large and small. Players take turns guessing grid coordinates at which they hope their opponent has hidden a boat. Correct guesses are like torpedoes that eventually win the game. There is no interaction between the two grids, so the grids are disassociated from each other. The game is each player racing independently to sink his opponent's boats before his own boats get sunk. The rules can specify that the game cannot end if one player has had more turns than the other, thus giving the imminent loser the full fairness of one last turn to achieve a tie.

Suppose Battleship players loathe the idea of a draw, and they say the first player to sink all boats wins. If it takes an average of perhaps 60 plies per player to win, then the normal range of plies needed by the winning player may be in the range of 46-74. With a normal range that wide, it will be relatively rare that both players take exactly the same number of plies to sink all their opponent's boats. By these odds Battleship tends to avoid draws.

Disassociation relieves any pressure to design the game with a reasonable balance between offense and defense. As long as offense usually over-powers defense, balance is not needed.

4. **Luck:** Most board games can eliminate the draw problem by introduction of raw luck. Many use dice. Poker uses shuffled hidden cards, and you never see a round of Poker end in a draw. Open minded or not, I would automatically reject the introduction of raw luck during a chess game as a means of reducing the draw problem, as would we all.

Let us not confuse the inclusion of chess960 initial setup randomization with any concept of luck. The setup selection process and outcome never favors either player over the other. Once the game begins there is no involvement of any random process or of anything else different from chess1.

5. **Asymmetry:** Asymmetries or imbalances seem to make for more decisive outcomes. Jeremy Silman has written about this extensively. The middle game can have a lot of symmetry when both players castle to the same wing. Highly symmetrical positions tend more often to end in a draw. Opposite wing castling creates what Jeremy Silman might call a positional imbalance, and imbalances lead to fewer draws.

This is where the OWC rule comes in. The simple idea is that more options for opposite wing castling should make it more popular. The resulting asymmetry would likely lead to a lower rate of draws. Since in chess1 a king can castle to square g1, it does not seem an outlandish idea that the king could instead castle to f1 or h1 or b1.

6
FEN and Chess960

FEN: Forsyth Edwards Notation
PGN: Portable Game Notation
UCI: Universal Chess Interface

How is a chess game represented to a chess software program? The dominant format is the simple textual format PGN (such as YourFileName.PGN). Here is one game (R#229-S#314) taken from a Chess Tigers PGN file containing many games (I added the comment for illustration):

[Event "CCM5 - FiNet Open"]
[Site "Mainz"]
[Date "2005/8/11"]
[Round "1"]
[White "Bogojawlenskij"]
[Black "Krasenkow"]
[Result "0-1"]
[SetUp "1"]
[FEN "nqrkbbrn/pppppppp/8/8/8/8/PPPPPPPP/NQRKBBRN w KQkq - 0 1"]

1. c4 g6 2. Nb3 e5 3. f3 Be7 4. Bf2 f5 5. d4 Nf7 6. e4 fxe4 7. Qxe4 d6 8. h4
Bc6 9. d5 Bd7 10. g4 c6 11. Bg2 Nc7 12. O-O O-O 13. g5 Bf5 14. Qe2 cxd5 15. f4
dxc4 16. Qxc4 Ne6 17. Qb4 Nxf4 18. Ng3 Nxg2 19. Nxf5 gxf5 20. Kxg2 b6 21. Rfe1
Qb7+ 22. Kg1 Kh8 23. Qd2 Rxc1 24. Nxc1 Rg8 25. Kh2 h6 26. Qe2 {Any comments
inside curly brackets.} Bxg5 0-1

In this chapter we are mostly interested in the FEN line. Near the end it contains "/NQRKBBRN". This is the final part of the position description, which in this normal case is the start position. This portion is all capital letters, meaning it represents all White pieces. The letters are in the eighth '/' delimited section, so that means row 1 (seems odd to me, but the first section means row 8). Each "/8/" means 8 contiguous vacant squares for that row.

The FEN piece letters are always the English letters for the American and British names of the pieces. In their own hand written notation, German speaking players generally use T-S-L-D-B for rook-knight-bishop-queen-pawn (the K is the same). Formal FEN never uses T-S-L-D-B in any country, at least not inside PGN computer files.

Next is a 'w' to indicate White has the next move. Skip the "KQkq" for the moment. The next "-" means no pawn can currently execute a capture of another in passing. If the latest ply had been c75, then the dash would instead be "c6". The "0" means zero plies have occurred since the latest capture or pawn move (used for the fifty plair draw rule). The final "1" means the next ply will be part of plair number 1.

Castle Rights Indicators: Step back to the string "KQkq". This concerns castling. The uppercase letters refer to White, and the lowercase refer to Black. If there are any uppercase letters, that means White's king has not yet moved. The "K" means White's 'h' wing rook has not yet moved, while the "Q" means White's 'a' wing rook has not yet moved. That is all they mean. As the odd FEN case diagram shows, these notations do not actually mean White has at least the possibility of castling now or later (**D6.1**).

Notice in the whole PGN/FEN example above that the chess960 game is being described by the same notations that have long worked for chess1. This kind of backward compatibility is very desirable.

Full Backward Compatibility is Impossible: Unfortunately there are some legal positions in chess960 that cannot be expressed unambiguously when limited to the chess1 FEN notation. The reasons are illustrated by the following two examples.

R#544 NNBR-KRQB: Imagine a chess960 game from setup R#544. A demonstration game could legally go as follows (only bothering to show White's moves): b24 d24 f24 Bc1a3 Nb1c3 Nc3e4 Rf13 Rf3b Rb31 (**D6.2**). White retains the right to castle 'a' wing with his Rd1. White cannot castle with the rook he moved to b1.

R#528 NRBN-KRQB: The same visual position can be reached from setup R#528 (b1 and d1 pieces swapped compared to R#544). A game could go: b24 d24 f24 Bc1a3 Nd1c3 Nc3e4 Rf13 Rf3d Rd31 (same **D6.2**). The difference is that White retains the right to castle 'a' wing later with his Rb1, and he cannot castle with his Rd1.

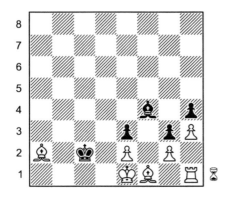

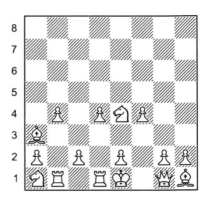

D6.1 Odd FEN case.

This odd position is legal and possible in chess1. FEN would notate White's castling eligibilities as "K", even though by circumstance it is fully impossible that White could castle during the rest of this game.

D6.2 After either 9. Rb31 or Rd31.
From R#544 & R#528.
X-FEN: "kDq" & "kQq" respectively.
Shredder-FEN: "fDd" & "fBb" respectively.

From chess960 diagram **D6.2** alone, we cannot determine whether the Rb1 or Rd1 is the rook eligible to castle. This shows the FEN specifications for chess1 are no longer adequate when chess960 is added, because here "kQq" is ambiguous. To interpret the "Q" correctly we would need to review the earlier moves and the start position (an unacceptable burden).

Fixing FEN

Old X-FEN: Reinhard Scharnagl had proposed an enhanced specification named X-FEN (formerly FRC-FEN; or why not FEN960?). X-FEN works by adding column letters where necessary to disambiguate. For instance, in the above R#544 case, the X-FEN castling state string would be "kQdq". The added 'd' in the substring "Qd" means White can castle 'a' wing using the rook on column 'd'. For the R#528 case it would be "kQbq". So old X-FEN uses two letters where, but only where, using only one letter is ambiguous.

There is a complication to explain. Scharnagl specified that in X-FEN, the disambiguating column letter should be omitted from the castling state string whenever the eligible rook is in the corner. The idea was to minimize the notation changes in order to maximize the degree of backward compatibility between the new specification and both (a) older chess software and (b) the PGN files already created for chess960.

Improved X-FEN: In late 2005 Scharnagl made two improvements to X-FEN (see chessbox.de/, file xfen_e.html). The first improvement is a simplification. For the R#544 case, Scharnagl now says "kQdq" should instead be "kDq". The "Qd" is replaced by "D", and no longer are two letters needed where classic FEN needed only one. Here the 'D' indicates White is allowed to castle with his 'd' column rook.

The second improvement to X-FEN increased its backward compatibility to FEN. For the R#528 case, we might think the X-FEN castling rights string would be "kBq". The 'B' is not backward compatible. So Scharnagl now specifies that the string would be "kQq". The reason is that he has adjusted his old idea that we use the classic letters K,Q,k,q only when the eligible rook is on a *corner* square. Now we use the classic letters K,Q,k,q whenever the eligible rook is the one *furthest* from the king on that side of the king. In the R#528 case the eligible Rb1 is further from the Ke1 than is the ineligible Rd1, so 'Q' will be used instead of 'B'.

A Small Disagreement in the Chess960 Community: With this improvement Scharnagl also may be doing what he can to solve a small argument that has occurred in the chess960 software world. There has been a debate about whether FEN should be replaced by X-FEN or by Shredder-FEN. Scharnagl's improved X-FEN moves closer to Shredder-FEN, in addition to increasing backward compatibility to FEN.

Shredder-FEN: Stefan Meyer-Kahlen is the developer of the high quality chess engine named Shredder. Shredder competed in the Mainz 2005/08 computer chess960 tournament. Through Shredder, Meyer-Kahlen has favored a more direct and simpler castling state string, one that names only the rooks that have not yet moved. The rooks are named by their start and still current column. Thus when starting a new chess960 game, for the traditional R#362 setup Shredder-FEN would use "HAha", and for R#528 it would use "FBfb".

To deal with the backward incompatibility of Shredder-FEN, it was also proposed that an additional UCI command be specified. So there would be FEN for chess1 and Shredder-FEN for chess960, rather than just one X-FEN to cover both. (See AaronTay.per.sg/Winboard/, file Winboard1.html. See also ShredderChess.com, file Download.html.)

Which Trade-off is Better?:   X-FEN is burdened with complications.   X-FEN has castling rights letters that vary during the game.   X-FEN has the caveat about the furthest rook from the king on the same side of the king.   But X-FEN maximizes backward compatibility.   Its unsolvable imperfection is rarely an issue in practice.

Shredder-FEN would have been the ideal choice many years ago when PGN and FEN were first invented.   It would have worked perfectly and simply for chess1, and no changes would be needed for chess960.   Realistically there was no way to foresee chess960 and the issues it brings, and "KkQq" seemed sufficient.

From my experiences in the software industry, it is rare to see anyone regret maintaining backward compatibility.   But in this situation full backward compatibility is not possible.   It is a judgment call as to the value of partial backward compatibility in this case.   The proposed addition of another UCI command might be seen as a kind of backward incompatibility too.

In 2005 the Chess Tigers published PGN files in both formats.   That was a wise decision, as their accommodating stance helped make the event compelling for a large number of entrants.   But the best long term policy is another matter.   I have chosen not to state in this book my judgment about which argument is stronger.

What Does Chess960 Software Do Today?:   Arena 1.1 seems unable to emit anything newer than the old chess1 FEN. So Arena 1.1 emits ambiguous PGN files, in these rare cases (as of late 2005).   Fritz9 emits Shredder-FEN.   For instance, in the R#544 (= F#728) case described above, Fritz9 emits "Dfd" (same as "fDd").   It remains to be seen how the PGN FEN specification will eventually settle.   The competitive commercial marketplace can only do so much to settle such issues, and it can sometimes settle them a certain way for the wrong reason.   Organizations like FIDE and USCF may have a role to play here.

Coordinate Notation for Castling in Chess960

In chess1 the ply O-O is expressed in coordinate notation to some chess software, as e1g1. The engine detects that this move is illegal except as a castling move, so it deduces that the player is castling. But in chess960 f1g1 could be a castling move or a legal king move. The question arises as to how castling moves should be expressed in coordinate notation for chess960?

I have seen two proposals. The trade-offs between these will be reminiscent of what we have just seen for FEN.

Proposal 1 – Exceptions Only: One proposal is to make no changes except for moves that would otherwise be ambiguous. If the king castles by moving two or more squares, then that should be the notated move. Thus moving the king f1c1 is easily understood to be a chess960 castling move. Now consider the ambiguous case where the king moves f1g1, when g1 is vacant and a rook is on h1. Here the notation shall be interpreted to be a plain king move not involving castling. If it could be a legal move of just the king, then it is not a castling move. To indicate castling, the king must be moved to the square currently occupied by the rook chosen for castling, as in f1h1. This is plainly illegal and it involves the rook, so the engine understands it is castling.

Proposal 2 - Always: The other proposal is to have the king always move to the square currently occupied by the rook chosen for castling. For the traditional chess1 or setup R#362 this would mean 'h' wing castling notation should be e1h1. The illegality and rook involvement of this move signals the intention to castle. Proposal 2 is less backward compatible than is 1, for coordinate notation.

Touch Move: Proposal 2 could be adapted as advice on how to safely negotiate the touch move rule when castling in chess960. Begin by taking your rook with your king. Continue by placing the two pieces on their destination squares, without worry over further touch move technicalities.

PGN Variant?: There is talk of adding to the PGN specification a line like one of the following. Some feel it would help, others feel it harms backward compatibility as is unnecessary anyway:

[Variant "chess960"]
[Variant "chess 960"]
[Variant "Fischerandom"]

Fritz9 adds [Variant "chess 960"], which seems odd to me since nobody else puts a space between chess and 960.

Part 2

New Chess Principles Discovered

"What is beyond dispute is that at all levels playing a few games of Fischerandom every now and again can improve our understanding of standard chess, in particular by giving us a greater grasp of how to coordinate our pieces and how to develop them to their strongest squares."

- The British magazine Chess, *May 2004, page 51*

Like everyone else did, I much enjoyed reading John Watson's acclaimed *Secrets of Modern Chess Strategy: Advances Since Nimzowitsch.* A significant portion of the book emphasizes the limitations of the traditional chess principles. The topic is addressed in a superbly comprehensive fashion, and a multitude of insightful observations are given. In one section Watson discusses how modern grandmasters have slowly become more willing to advance the pawns in front of their castled king. Consensus thinking on this topic has changed relatively recently, since the era of Alekhine. During my studies of chess960 I realized this transformation of thought would have occurred earlier in chess history if chess960 had been in vogue. There are some things about fundamental chess that we can learn more efficiently from chess960 than from chess1.

I mention Watson's book because here in this book we next begin a novel approach to assessing the principles of chess. Some new principles and techniques will be described. Some long standing principles will be questioned even further than has already been the case in books about chess1. The end result for us will be a deeper understanding of both the chess pieces and the chess board. This kind of knowledge transcends the particular rule set we might use in any given chess game. This knowledge could be beneficial to anyone playing either chess1 or chess960.

In the chess1 literature about principles of strong play, there is the implicit assumption that the principles flow from fundamental chess, from considerations of the individual pieces and the board. By examining chess960 I have concluded that some of the principles derive in part from the mere particulars of the chess1 setup. Some of those principles look weaker when put to the test with a wider variety of initial setups. Comprehending which principles those are, and why they are less broadly applicable than assumed, can deepen our understanding of Caissa's unbiased chess.

In this part of the book it will be argued that the effects of the setup are more pervasive than even the chess960 community has recognized. Of course the opening phase is greatly affected. But I found that both the middle game and even the endgame are affected by the particulars of the setup. I suspect there is variation by setup in the relative values of the pieces (especially knights and bishops) during the opening phase and early middle game phase, though this book does not delve into that.

7

Strategies for the Modified Setup Phase

There are four phases to any chess game. Phases two through four are well known as the opening, the middle game, and the endgame. We have never before called it by a name, but I call the first phase the setup phase.

In the chess1 realm the setup phase has not been recognized as a phase at all. This is because the chess1 setup never varies the way it does in chess960. In chess1 we instead talk about opening "theory", referring to the accumulation of at-home pre-game calculation and analysis of the chess1 setup position. As part of the chess1 setup phase we also have the devised opening principles given by Aron Nimzovich in his *My System*, which was also written at home. The setup phase is different in chess960. Yes there can be at-home thought and preparations as part of the chess960 setup phase (as this book should demonstrate). But in chess960 the setup phase comes alive and requires original thought in real time, in the several minutes after the pieces are set but before the clocks are started. This chapter is devoted to the topic of handling those pre-game minutes.

With this chapter we begin our technical examination of how to play stronger chess960 moves on the board. We will search for a logical system that can bring order to what can otherwise seem like an unstructured chaotic initial setup of pieces behind pawns. From order we may have a plausible opportunity to begin the long process of determining stronger opening play in chess960.

Do the Chess1 Opening Principles of Nimzovich Remain True for Chess960?

Suppose a brief ten minutes ago you and your opponent were given the chess960 setup you must use in your tournament game. You have never seen this setup before. If you are new to chess960 the setup looks unruly and chaotic to you. It will soon be time for you to make the first move as White. How do you determine a quality move to play?

Mimic Chess1: Perhaps one approach would be to play as close to a known chess1 opening as the setup allows. If you like the Ruy Lopez, open 1. e24 2. N-f3 (if possible) etc. If you like the Queen's Gambit, open 1. d24 etc. Obviously this approach would be doomed and even silly. Maybe an opening like the Reti, 1. N-f3 if possible, might be a plausible concept in many chess960 setups, but that really just delays the question until plair 2.

There is always the symmetrical approach to opening with Black, as in the spirit of the chess1 Petroff Defense, for example: **1. e24 e75 2. Ng1f3 Ng8f6 3. Nf3:e5 Nf6:e4 4. Qd1e2 Qd8e7 5. Qe2:4 d76 6. d24 d6:Ne5 7. d4:e5 Nb8c6 8. Bf1b5.** It will usually lead to a disadvantage for Black to answer each White ply with the equivalent mirror ply, waiting for the plair when continuing the symmetry would cause disaster.

Classic Chess Opening Principles: A more reasonable approach would be to use the very general principles beginners learn for chess1 openings, the principles enunciated by Nimzovich. I like the way Reuben Fine restated these ideal principles in his *Chess the Easy Way*. Of course, these ideals might not all be achievable in every game. Here I may slightly alter Fine's wording, mostly to eliminate the chess1 bias.

1. Open by advancing a center column pawn.

2. Prefer developing moves that also create a threat against the opponent. Knights are best for this.

3. Develop knights before bishops.

4. Develop each piece to the square best for it, then leave it there until opening development is completed.

5. Make one or two pawn moves in the opening, not more.

6. Do not bring your queen out early.

7. Castle as soon as possible, preferably toward the 'h' wing.

8. Play to get control of the center.

9. Always try to maintain at least one pawn in the center.

Now, do these venerated recommendations qualify as fundamental principles of chess, or are they merely principles of the chess1 setup position? After examining chess960, I believe some of these principles apply well to both chess1 and to all of the chess960 setups. However, the other principles on this list are of lesser stature. They work for chess1, but they are limited to chess1 and a handful of other similar setups. They are context sensitive principles, brittle, not always broadly applicable to chess regardless of the initial position.

Indiscriminant obedience to these principles could be outright harmful in some chess960 setups.

I see this realization as harmonious with John Watson's central thesis, that best possible play is guided by the particulars of the given position rather than by general principles. We know the chess1 setup is a 'position', but we rarely say so explicitly. The static nature of the chess1 setup led to a confound in the perspective available to Nimzovich when he formulated his opening principles. I wonder whether Nimzovich explicitly thought in terms of the distinction drawn here, between principles dependent on the particular chess1 setup versus fundamental principles of chess that apply well regardless of how the pieces are arranged behind the pawns. Either way, the fact that about half of his opening principles do apply well to all chess960 setups shows us some truths. First, Nimzovich was successful at penetrating into the foundation of the general chess opening phase. Second, it shows us that chess960 is just chess: even radical rearrangements of the rank 1 pieces are subject to some of these same opening principles. This is a counter-balance to anyone who might go too far in rejecting any role for principles in chess play. Third, it is harder to fully understand chess opening principles when restricting oneself to chess1 and rejecting consideration of chess960.

Next we reassess each classic opening principle in the context of chess960.

Principle 1 (central pawn): This principle has been routinely disobeyed by grandmasters playing chess960 at Mainz. For many setups the data show grandmasters judge it more effective to open with wing pawns. Sometimes the advancing of central column pawns is long delayed. Wing pawn openings happen at a much higher rate in some setups than they do in others like the chess1 setup.

Principle 2 (threaten): This principle is partly true for chess960. Who can argue with the idea of threatening the enemy and forcing him to react. This fits chess960 to the same degree it fits chess1, or maybe even better. Chess960 sometimes offers opportunities to create a threat with White's first ply, which is never possible in chess1. Yet this principle may have less ability to generate specific moves for other more positional openings. It occurs to me that the threat idea in principle is so fundamental that it might apply well to board games other than chess.

The second phrase of this principle does not fit chess960 well. In chess1 the bishops and queen are not well placed for immediate attack, but in several chess960 setups they are. The chess960 games played in Mainz consistently show that in certain setups knights are not the best pieces for generating early threats. Knights are not long range pieces. Bishops that start near a corner are often the first to make threats. Knights that start in a corner are usually too far from the center to make early threats.

Principle 3 (knights first): In certain classes of chess960 setups, grandmasters playing in Mainz routinely activate their bishops before activating their knights. Among the very few chess960 master games thus far published, we already have games where the first knight move occurs long after we consistently see the first knight move in chess1 (the opening of this game will be shown later).

Nimzovich wrote "A Pawn move must not in itself be regarded as a developing move, but merely as an aid to development". This is sound for the chess1 setup, but we cannot adopt it for all setups. This does not work for setups where a bishop or queen starts on a corner square.

We frequently see wing pawn opening moves, like 1. b23, when a bishop starts in a corner. Technically this is not a move of the bishop, but that is the spirit of the move. The intention of the move has nothing to do with controlling square c4. In chess1 the common 1. e24 is as much about fighting for the four center squares as it is about discovering the Bf1.

Principle 4 (move once): Chess960 and chess1 play should equally benefit from the advice to get most or all pieces developed or activated before moving any developed piece a second time.

Principle 5 (two pawns): Nimzovich encouraged restraint against making too many pawn moves before the pieces were developed. For chess960 the jury is still out on this one. From replaying chess960 games from Mainz, I have an intuition that many chess960 setups are better suited to more pawn moves during the opening phase than is the chess1 setup. It may be necessary to make early advances of central pawns plus pawns on both wings, in certain setups.

Consider setup R#571-S#368 BBNR-KRNQ. Here pawn advances are required on the 'a' wing. The Qh1 will have to be brought nearer to the central columns, perhaps being freed by g23. Even hypermodern opening devotees hope to eventually advance their central column pawns under favorable conditions.

My theorizing notwithstanding, I could not find good evidence to support making a claim that some chess960 setups lure more opening phase pawn moves than does chess1.

Principle 6 (queen): Nimzovich's principle against early queen activity might be harmful advice in some chess960 setups. In chess1 the Qd1 is optimally placed for best usage of her strengths. From d1 the queen can provide defensive force to the lighter pieces that advance the front lines to engage the enemy. When d1 is not the best vantage point to provide that defense, d1 is at least a central starting point from which she can usually reach the necessary square. The lesson from chess1 is to let other pieces begin the battle, and delay moving the queen until a specific reason arises.

The situation is different in some chess960 setups. There are plenty of setups where the queen starts far from the center. Should that have any effect on the way advances are made with the lighter pieces, or with the pawns? I would be surprised if the answer was always no. There are probably fewer options for pressing with the lighter pieces when the queen cannot provide backing support. Thus there may be substantial motive in chess960 to move the queen early, to reposition her toward the central columns. In chess1 the queen may sit on its initial d1 square well into the middle game, but that does not mean she is uninvolved. In chess960, an unmoved queen still sitting on h1 may indeed be insufficiently involved, and she represents a lot of force to have out of play. Early moves may be well spent on relocating the queen off of h1.

Principle 7 (castle): The classic principles about castling apply in chess960, but not quite as well as they do in chess1. There are setups where it appears to be plausible to forego castling, where the king may be just as safe staying in the center as he would be jumping to either wing. This situation arises in setups where wing pawn advances have ruined the defensive potential castling. The center is rarely a safe place for the king, but in some setups the wings end up being no safer.

In chess960 there are many setups where the king starts on his castling destination square, perhaps removing part of the standard motivation for castling. It will be interesting to see over time whether castling is less frequent in setups where the king starts on b1 or g1.

A fascinating aspect of some chess960 setups is the dilemmas posed for castling when queens or bishops start in the corners. Consider the case of adjacent bishops on a1,b1. The 'a' wing pawns must advance to activate the bishops. Castling to the 'a' wing may be made unsafe by those pawn advances. Yet castling to the other wing would locate your king directly in the sights of the enemy bishops. Might the central columns be the safest place for the king to stay? We will look at some relevant games later.

King safety aside, there remains the need to connect the two rooks. We will likely see castling being used to unite the rooks even in positions where the king may have preferred to remain uncastled.

When castling does occur in chess960, my data analyses will show a preference for castling to the wing on which the king started.

Principle 8 (center): Both chess1 and chess960 use the same chess board. The board dictates that the center, meaning primarily the four squares d4,d5,e4,e5, are at the crucial midpoint of the most important lines of communication and coordination. Thus this principle of controlling the center applies equally well to all chess960 setups, including the traditional R#362. Only the optimal methods of control will vary by setup.

Principle 9 (pawn center): During the 1920's the theory of the hypermodern approach to controlling the center became a major topic. The basic idea was to delay advancing your own central pawns to rank 4, and to aim your pieces at the opponent's advanced central pawns (such as with fianchettoed bishops). When conditions were right, often a player would attack the opponent's center pawns with c24. That provoked a favorable exchange of wing pawn for center pawn, or it compelled the opponent to advance to his pawn to rank 5 where it would be even harder to defend.

The hypermodern theory was ultimately deemed inferior. In my view most theories, in chess and in science and all other realms, are eventually overthrown by refined theories or entirely new concepts. This does not mean the overthrown theories should be seen as failures. Rather they provided a structured starting point for others to organize new findings to achieve a better theory. Chess masters gained a better understanding of pawn center strengths and weaknesses from the work done to challenge the hypermodern approach.

In many chess960 setups with cornered bishops, there is an obvious potential for reconsidering the hypermodern approach, because it can be implemented with fewer plies. Though the data is as yet sparse, there is evidence to support the suspicion that some setups do sway grandmasters to an extreme form hypermodern opening play (as will be shown later). Chess960 may bring us a broader variety of theoretical styles, which might further advance or accelerate our understanding of fundamental chess principles.

Dealing with Complexity: Chess1 was invented in 1475. It was over four centuries later that Aron Nimzovich published the first comprehensive articulation of the opening principles every club player now takes for granted. That was with just one initial setup to consider. Now we have 959 more. We have seen that some of the chess1 opening principles apply less well to some other setups, but to which setups in particular?

We can imagine a large two dimensional table of data, with the nine chess1 opening principles labeling the columns across the top, and the 960 setups labeling the rows down the left edge. In each of the 8640 cells we could assess the degree to which the principle was good advice for the associated setup. But rules do not permit us to view that table after the setup is announced. We are not going to expect players to memorize 8640 cells. A simple method of abstraction and reduction must be devised.

In the next section of this chapter, I describe the scheme I created to clarify the application of chess opening principles to any particular chess960 setup. In chess960 tournaments the setup is revealed only minutes before the start of each round. So the scheme needs to be exercisable within those few minutes.

Rationalization of Setups: How?

Let us begin the inevitable process of trial and error. If we could find a way to categorize the 960 setups, we might then be able to determine what principles apply to each category. Then in the minutes before our tournament chess960 games begin, we could determine the category of the randomly chosen setup, and we could follow the opening principles known to fit that category. How shall we categorize the setups?

Intrinsic Setups: One simplifying reduction of setups we can attempt is to work with the 480 intrinsic setups (one per reciprocal pair) instead of all 960 setups. The number 480 is still far more than the 1 setup in chess1. So by itself this reduction does not solve the problem.

Gligoric's FRC book (page 80) shows that the reduction to intrinsic setups can be a risky over simplification. Consider the setup reciprocal-pair containing the chess1 setup of R#362. The reciprocal Ruy Lopez Open variation does not translate well from R#362 to R#862. Problems arise from the difference in destination squares for a king and chosen rook castling to the 'a' wing. Consider that in R#862-S#534 RNBK-QBNR, **1. d24 d75 Nb1c3 Ng8f6 3. Bc1g5 h76 4. Bg5h4 Nb8c6 5. Kd1c/Rad Nc6:d4??** simply no longer works for Black. So the idea of simplifying to 480 setups for analysis can lead to mistakes born from over-simplification. However, it is not clear that the castling wing asymmetry would harm all or even most chess1 openings in an analogous manner. Further, it was pre-game calculations that told us the asymmetry would be a problem in R#862, but for other setups we do not have such information available.

One-to-Many Categorization is Impossible: The next natural way to reduce the size of the problem is to try grouping bunches of similar setups into categories. The idea would be to put each setup into one of perhaps a dozen categories. Well, what would those categories be? Let us brainstorm some candidate categories to see what they might feel like:

- One corner bishop
- Two corner bishops
- Bishops adjacent in the center
- King in the center
- King on a wing
- Queen in the center
- Queen in a corner
- One rook in the center
- Centralized rooks both adjacent to the king
- Knights having one ply access to c3 and f3

It quickly becomes apparent that no one-to-many categorization of setups is possible. If a setup has a king on the wing, two corner bishops, and one rook in the center, then to which one category should we assign the setup? There can be no clear answer when limited to a one-to-many hierarchical taxonomy. We could establish a many-to-many relationship between setup category and each individual setup, but then the whole system would break down when we try to assign distinctive ideas to each category. Either there is too much overlap between categories, or too many categories, or most setups need to be in multiple categories. Our supposedly reduced numerical product would have to be re-expanded beyond manageable limits. This approach of setup categorization is a failure. Another approach is needed.

List of Setup Attributes

To understand the chess960 setups we need a study scheme with more granularity than the traditional chess1 opening principles can provide. Yet the scheme must avoid generating so many cases that it becomes impractical to use. The scheme I have devised is driven by the concept of setup attributes. I have created a short list of attributes. Each setup has values for most or all of the attributes on the list. The scheme I have devised provides the list of attributes, and explains how to quickly determine the value of each attribute in any given setup. Before your chess960 game begins you will need only a few minutes to perform this simple cataloging. In the next chapter we will describe how to use this cataloged information to derive the basic themes you then use to guide your opening plies. Of course, this cataloging scheme can be applied to the chess1 setup no less than to any other.

List of Attributes: Here is the list of attributes to be assessed for any given setup:

Undefended rank 2 pawns.	
	Which are at risk for first ply or early attack? Pa2 Pb2 Pg2 Ph2 are easier for enemy bishops and queen to attack early from afar than are Pd2 Pe2.
Undefended rank 4 squares.	
	Which are at risk for first ply attack, if occupied with a pawn?
	Thus which adjacent pawn may need to move to rank 3 to defend the rank 4 pawn?

Corner piece mobilization plans.	
	Q: Which mobilization theme seems best?
	N: Which mobilization theme seems best?
	B: Does this bishop have a covered attack on the opposing corner piece that is unrequited? If yes, is that opposing piece defended?
King fort.	
	Do you hope to castle?
	Design if castling 'a' side?
	Design if castling 'h' side?
Is there knight opposition?	
	Do both White knights start on the same shade of square? If yes, then perhaps no knight opposition. See later chart.
Hypermodern or central pawn advance?	
	Which pawns am I willing to block on rank 2 with pieces I develop to rank 3?

Explanation of Setup Attributes

At this point the reader may want to have a chess board and pieces handy while reading.

Undefended rank 2 pawns:

In the static chess1 setup R#362-S#518 RNBQ-KBNR each rank 2 pawn is defended. Also, there is no first ply that can attack an opposing pawn. But in setup R#694-S#079 NNRK-QRBB each player starts with two undefended pawns, in columns a-b. Further, those a-b pawns can be attacked by the opponent's first ply. These pawns are not hard to defend. Yet if White begins the game by attacking those pawns, then Black may have an unusually large inherent disadvantage simply because he must use his earliest plies to defend his pawns (or resort to a symmetrical counter-attack down a tempo). This kind of setup may emphasize the undesirable aspects of the arbitrary unfair first move rule that so favors White.

Starting from R#694, a fool's mate involving the undefended Pb7 could go **1. Na1b3 g75 2. Nb3a5 Bh8:b2 3. Na5:b7##**. In the grandmaster chess960 games from Mainz there are many middle game attacks that exploit weaknesses in the enemy's rank 2. Players are not yet used to these rank 2 weakness patterns that are omitted by chess1.

For R#694, a more realistic opening sequence we might see at the club level, with constant threats by White, is **1. g24 Nb8c6 2. f24 a76 3. Qe1f2 Na8b6 (threat was 4. Bh1:Nc6 d7:Bc6 5. Qf2a7, (D7.1)**. White has played all forcing moves to open the game, in accordance with Nimzovich's opening principle 2. White has the only advanced pawn presence on the board, White has three pieces pouring heat across at the enemy, and White has the next move. However, Black has two pieces developed in his first three plies, and Black has a well defended king fort available now on the 'a' wing. As I discuss elsewhere, the king will usually need to castle away from his own cornered adjacent bishop pair (or resort to a king fort of pieces like Bh1g2 Bg1f2 K-g1/Rf).

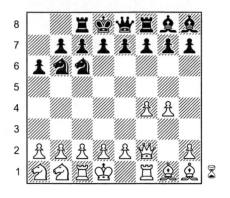

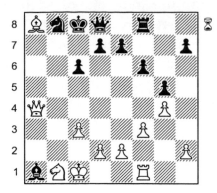

D7.1 R#694 after 3. Qe1f2 Na8b6.
Defending against White's
aggressive opening moves.

D7.2 R#694 after 11. Qd1a4.
Defeating Black's symmetrical opening,
and winning material.

In sharp attacking setups like R#694 Black should consider whether to adopt a defensive stance, or instead a very sharp counter-attacking stance. The counter-attack is usually achieved by playing symmetrical opening plies (like in the traditional Petroff Defense). Next is one possible example from R#694:

1.	g24	g75	2.	Bh1:b7	Bh8:b2	3.	Bb7:Na8	Bb2:Na1
4.	Kd1c/Rcd	Kd8c/Rcd	5.	c23	c76	6.	f23	f76
7.	Bg1:a7	Bg8:a2	8.	Ba7b6	Ba2b3	9.	Bb6:Rd8	Bb3:Rd1
10.	Qe1:Bd	Qe8:Bd	11.	Qd1a4 (D7.2)				

The symmetrical moves sequence is broken by the impending interaction of the queens.

Undefended rank 4 squares.

In R#694 the only rank 4 squares in Black territory that are considered undefended by Black are a5 and g5. Black defends square b5 with his Qe1 after d76, square f5 with his Rf8 after f75, and so on.

In R#692-S#075 NNRK-BQRB White may have some planning to do before he could seek to control the center through pawn occupation. White has no piece defending d4. If the game opens **1. d24 g76 2. Na1b3 Nb8c6**, White could reply **3. e23 (D7.3)**, but that defensive Philidor-looking move does not seem to maintain any advantage of first move for White. White could open 1. e24 but that would immediately block his potentially powerful Bh1.

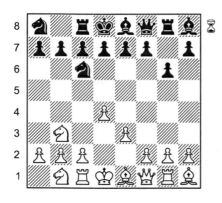

D7.3 R#692. After 3. e23

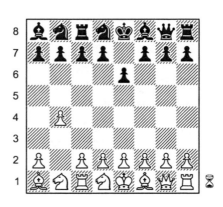

D7.4 R#690. After 1... e76. White must spend a tempo defending Pb4.

R#690-S#162 BNRN-KBQR could begin **1. b24 e76 (D7.4)**, where the unprotected state of the Pb4 may cost White a valuable tempo early in the game, probably for 2. a23. Thus 1. b23 might be better for White. If instead we swap positions of the Rc1-with-Nb1 to make the setup R#674-S#450 BRNN-KBQR, the initial ply of 1. b24 might be more attractive, since the Rb1 protects square b4.

Corner piece mobilization plans.

There are interesting issues that arise over how to mobilize various pieces that might be setup on a corner square. Static chess1 never gives us any opportunity to enjoy tackling these issues. The issues arise from the following considerations:

- Should corner knights be developed as early as knights are in chess1? After one move out of the corner a knight influences only half as many of the precious four center squares as in chess1. Maybe there is less urgency?

- A Black bishop on h8 may have a more difficult task in getting activated or developed by discovery (as in g76) than its White counterpart on a1, due to 1. b23 giving White an initiative. This situation interacts with whether the g8 piece defends Bh8 (as would a Rg8 or Qg8, but not Bg8).

- Developing a corner queen diagonally is popular when the other attributes of the setup make it plausible. Even with a Rg8 defending it, the valuable Qh8 cannot counterpunch a White Ba1 with 1. b23 g76.

- In chess1 our queen need not and even should not be developed early. But that is not to say the queen therefore is a good fit for remaining long on a corner square in chess960.

Corner Knights: About 44% of all chess960 setups have at least one knight in a corner. The grandmaster games from Mainz show a preference for making the first move of corner knight to rank 3 over rank 2. In a setup with Bf1 and Nh1, where the fianchetto Bf1g2 is foreseen, the move g23 is probably not as strong as g24, if Pg4 can be supported.

A knight (or bishop) in the corner compels us to ask whether there is a threat to the pawn in front (such as Bh8 & Ph7). When Black has Nh8 and Rg8, and when White has Bb1, the Black Ph7 may need to consume an early ply for protection. The Nh8 can defend Ph7 by Nh8g6 blocking the diagonal threat, but that leaves the knight pinned and thus less active.

By winning the Mainz chess960 open twice in two attempts, in 2003 and again in 2005, Levon Aronian has established himself as a chess960 celebrity. In 2003 Peter Svidler won the Mainz chess960 champion title away from Peter Leko, and Svidler has continued to successfully defend it. As of 2005/08 both Aronian and Svidler were ranked in the chess1 top 10 worldwide by FIDE. In 2005/10 Svidler tied for second in the FIDE Championship tournament in San Luis, Argentina. Thus the repeated successes of Aronian and Svidler in chess960 underscore the correctness of asserting that chess960 is just chess. The continuing annual participation of these and other chess1 elites suggests an eventual rise of chess960 to a higher status.

In Mainz 2005/08 round 1, Aronian and Ferdinand Niebling faced setup R#229-S#314 NQRK-BBRN. This setup has four corner knights. Through the first 14 plies there had still been no knight moves. Even the rooks had advanced beyond rank 1. After 20 minutes of casual looking through my own books and database, I failed to find any chess1 game where the first knight move came so late as in their game.

L.Aronian – F.Niebling, R#229

1.	c24	g76	2.	g24	e75	3.	f24	Bf8c5
4.	Be1h4#	Bc5e7	5.	Bh4:Be7#	Kd8:Be7	6.	f4:e5	c75
7.	Rg13	Rc86 (D7.5)	8.	Na1b3!	Na8c7	9.	Bf1g2	Rc6e
10.	Nb3:c5	Re6:5	11.	d24	Re5:Nc	12.	d4:Rc5	Nc7e6

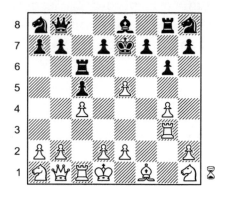

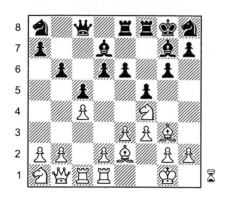

D7.5 R#229. L.Aronian – F.Niebling.
After 7. Rg13 Rc86.
No knight moves yet.

D7.6   R#229. E.Bacrot – J.Beutel.
After 13. Nb3a1 Nc7a8.
Only one knight not on its setup square.

In the other R#229 games knight moves came earlier, though it was common that one player or the other would make no knight moves until the fifth plair. In E.Bacrot – J.Beutel, Black's first knight move occurred as 12... Na8c7, and the next two plies were to un-develop knights back into the corners with 13. Nb3a1 Nc7a8 (**D7.6**).

When first moves of the corner knights do come, roughly 64% of them are to rank 3 not rank 2. For reasons yet unknown, in R#933-S#897 BRKB-QRNN (2005) all but one first move of a corner knight was to rank 3, in stark contrast to the other setups I tallied.

Corner Queen: The queen is the most powerful piece in chess by virtue of her exceptional mobility. So it is ironic that the queen often needs help from her teammates to get liberated from the corner to a more effective square. A player would ideally like to develop by discovery his corner queen, but this is not always plausible. The problem with the queen is that it cannot fight with bishops along the long diagonal, because the bishop is only too happy to exchange itself off for the enemy queen.

In R#626-S#946 BRKR-NBNQ with 1. b23 Black may have difficulty liberating or centralizing his Qh8. Over the course of the first dozen plairs Black may include moves like Ng8f6 g76 Bf8g7 Qh8f (**D7.7**). Or maybe h75 Qh86 would be better liberating moves. Or there is always 1. b23 b76 as an approach by Black.

Consider the game A.Yusupov - L.Nisipeanu, R#155 - S#393 QRNB-BNKR, Round 3, Mainz 2003/08. Both players faced the problem of getting their queen from the 'a' corner to the 'h' wing. The players chose different routes (**D7.8**):

White: a24, b23, Qa1d, Qd12, Qd2g.
Black: a75, b76, Qa8c6, Qc6e8, Qe8g6.

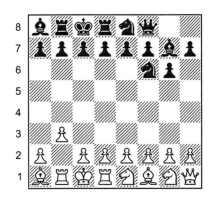
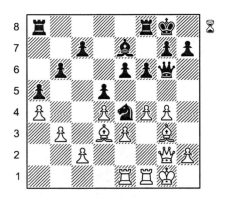

D7.7 R#626. Black tries to centralize his queen with Qh8f.

D7.8 R#155. Yusupov – Nisipeanu After 21. Qd2g, queens reach 'g'.

Corner Bishop: A corner bishop is a built-in incentive to consider using the hypermodern approach to controlling the four center squares. In 7% of the setups the two bishops will both pressure the center along the corner diagonals. If we add the queen's diagonal force, then in 12% of the setups diagonal pressure will emanate from all corners. Early B:B exchanges often occur in setups where bishops occupy all four corners. The play from Mainz shows uncovering a corner bishop is usually the first priority in the early opening, not developing the knights.

When the randomly chosen setup has a knight in one corner and a bishop in the other, we sometimes see the corner knight invade enemy territory by hugging the edge of the board. Let us consider a setup that has Ba1 and Nh1. After moves b23 Nh1g3 Ng3h5, the g7 square deep in Black's half of the board is under coordinated attack. In Mainz, different grandmasters independently created and implemented this attack plan, with some success, even though the Nh5 is on the rim of the board.

In the days of WCC Wilhelm Steinitz, Siegbert Tarrasch's catchy rule "A knight on the rim is dim" carried the consensus of opinion. Informally many chess players added "And a knight in the corner is grim." John Watson wrote that modern masters give much less deference to this rule. In 1475 had the inventors of chess included setup variation among their many dramatic chess rule changes, there never would have been such a rule from Tarrasch. When a knight starts on h1, h5 is a square it can reach naturally as a way to penetrate into enemy territory, often with excellent coordination from it teammates, and often without immediate risk of being exchanged away. After a short time playing chess960 it becomes clear that there are several situations in which "A knight on the rim can win", at least when coordination with other pieces is involved. Again we see that chess960 can be a better teacher about what the pieces can do.

Corner Rook: All chess1 players know the rook is a piece which often plays no part in the opening, and sometimes no part until after the middle game is well underway. Beginners are told this is so because the rook is inherently a piece that cannot become mobile until after a couple pawns have been taken away to open up columns. Oddly, neither Nimzovich nor Fine stated any formal opening principle or rule for the rooks. The list of opening principles would have included one about the rooks if chess960 had been in vogue, because their style of usage varies by setup. In text Fine did write that rooks should be moved to columns where a pawn is missing.

When I review games from other chess960 setups I am unsure about whether the rooks are often playing more of a role in the opening. One observation implying they do comes from the sometimes frequent advances of pawns protected by a rook setup in or adjacent to the central columns d-e. Scanning the Mainz games I have tallied some data about the frequencies of 'c' pawn advances when there is versus is not a supporting rook setup on 'c'. After gathering the data I had no confidence in any conclusions I might draw from them. There are too many other factors that make each setup unique even though they might share a 'c' rook. From the pawn advance data then, no conclusion can yet be drawn about the possibly increased opening phase role of the rook in chess960.

Perhaps a better criterion would be a comparison of how soon any rook moves beyond rank 1. In this book I am never claiming any statistical analyses that are so rich with data that they are definitive. I am only casting light on some trends that seem to be occurring. I took 18 Mainz chess960 games in which at least one rook was setup on a column c-f, and I tallied the plair number in which any rook finally advanced beyond rank 1. Then I took 18 Mainz chess1 games and made the same tally (all games had the same G/20 +5 delay time control). The results were that the first rook advance occurred about 9 plies and 27% earlier in the chess960 games. This trend may be interesting, but may not go far enough to support an idea that in chess960 the non-corner rooks play a role earlier in the opening than rooks do in chess1.

King Fort

In most chess1 games it is highly advisable to castle. In chess960 there are some initial setups for which castling may be more optional. In some setups castling to one particular wing might be implausible. When an adjacent bishop pair starts in columns 'a' and 'b', it may be unsafe to castle 'a' side. The pawns on that wing must advance, meaning they cannot remain on rank 2 for king protection. Perhaps in chess960 we need to be more open to the concept of king forts comprised of pieces rather than of pawns (as in Ba1b2 Bb1c2 OOO). In chess1, king forts are built mostly from rank 2 pawns. So in such cases any castling would seem to be limited to 'h' side. Yet 'h' wing castling may be hindered by the queen being initially assigned to column 'g', and by the fact the enemy bishops are aimed at their opponent's 'h' wing. The data from grandmaster games may leave us in doubt about all of this.

Overall, immediately after the setup is announced, each player should determine whether castling options might be limited to one wing. If yes, then care should be taken against early pawn pushes on that wing. Advance planning during the setup phase may be needed to avoid such pawn pushes.

The trends in the Mainz chess960 play indicate that a high quality king fort is less of a priority than we are led to believe by the limited experiences chess1 allows us. In many games all the pawns in front of the castled king were advanced before castling occurred. Piece mobilization was the higher weighted priority. This is an instance where chess960 can teach us corrective adjustments in our understanding of the relative weights of middle game principles (not just opening principles). In most cases the poor quality king forts did not turn out to be a major weakness in the positions. This shows how deeply grandmasters understand chess positions, even positions in patterns never seen in chess1.

In chess1 there need not be any conflict between a high quality king fort and other major opening phase goals. Both goals are attainable due to the contrived nature of the static chess1 setup. We too rarely see games where both players have voluntarily dissipated their king forts for other strengths. It is interesting to watch games unfold with this unfamiliar set of priorities.

Knight Opposition

Due to the particulars of the chess1 setup and to the fact it never varies, we do not think of knights as having a light v. dark shade aspect anything like bishops have. But again, it is healthy to consider the possibility that our chess experiences have been harmfully limited by our exclusive adherence to chess1. For analyzing chess960 setups it is useful to gently apply the idea that each knight is either a light or dark knight, though only for the first portion of the game. These square shadings are central to a setup feature we can call "knight opposition". Some chess960 setups have knight opposition, strongly or weakly, while others have no knight opposition.

To over simplify a little, the test for knight opposition in a chess960 setup is to ask whether both White knights start on the same shade of square as each other. If same shade, then there is no knight opposition. If different shade, then there is either full, partial or no knight opposition. In chess1 there is always maximal knight opposition, as is shown in the next table. As a chess enthusiast, do you have any interest in knowing how the opening and middle game phases are affected when knight opposition is removed?

Knight Opposition in Setup

Columns Between Knights	Knights on Columns, Example	Full Opp	Partial Opp: High , Low	No Opp	Freq %
(diff shade)					*(60 %)*
0	de	-	Partial/H	-	26 %
2	c..f	-	Partial/L	-	19 %
4	b....g	Full	-	-	11 %
6	a......h	-	-	No Opp	4 %
(same shade)				*(No Opp)*	*(40 %)*
1	c.e	-	-	No Opp	20 %
3	c...g	-	-	No Opp	13 %
5	a.....g	-	-	No Opp	7 %

Different Shade Cases: 0/de: In the partial knight opposition case of knights on "0/de", consider 1. Ne1d3 Nd8c6 (D). Here Black's Nc6 is in proper position to exchange off knights should White decide to penetrate to one of the four center squares, as in 2. Nd3e5 Nc6:Ne5. However, if White is willing to settle for an enemy square adjacent to the four center square area, White can move 2. Nd3c5 unopposed. Black could have swapped his exchange potentials at e5 v. c5 by instead moving 1... Nd8e6, but Black cannot oppose both entry squares. Among circumstances of partial opposition, this "0/de" case rates relatively strong, because the correct center squares can be opposed.

We might consider "0/gh" to have a slightly higher degree of knight opposition, because a Nh1 does not have the option of avoiding the enemy knight by moving away from it (there is no 9th column 'i' for Nh1i3).

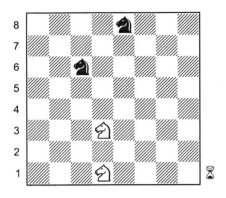

After 1. Ne1d3 Nd8c6.
Different shades. The "**0/de**" case.
Strong partial knight opposition (e5).

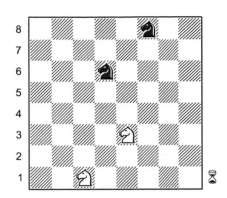

After 1. Nf1e3 Nc8d6.
Different shades. The "**2/cf**" case.
Weak partial knight opposition.
Better opposition if 1... Nc8e7.

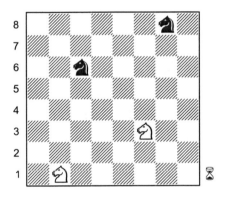

After 1. Ng1f3 Nb8c6.
Different shades. The "**4/bg**" case.
Full knight opposition.

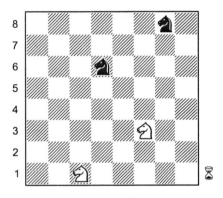

After 1. Ng1f3 Nc8d6.
Same shades. The "**3/cg**" case.
No knight opposition.

2/cf: In the "2/cf" case after 1. Nf1e3 Nc8d6 (**D**) White is prevented from playing 2. Ne3f5. More importantly though White has unhindered access to play the more valuable 2. Ne3d5. Yes Black can retort with the similar (albeit not exactly symmetric) 2... Nd6e4, but the current topic is narrowed to knight penetration potentials, not to what advantages it may bring. If Black is in a defensive mood he could play 1... Nc8b6 to hinder Ne3d5, but that may harm Black by taking his knight too far from the center of the battle. A better alternative to counter both Ne3d5 and Ne3f5 is 1... Nc8e7, though on rank 2 it cramps Black and puts no pressure on the center squares in White's territory.

4/bg: The "4/bg" case (**D**) is the only one that has full knight opposition. Full knight opposition is rare, occurring in only 11% of all chess960 setups. The chess1 setup is among this 11%, so we can see how unusual the chess1 setup is, even beyond the fact it is wing symmetric. I wonder whether setups with full knight opposition are inherently more draw prone than are other classes of setups? If so, then we might expect a lower rate of draws in chess960 compared to chess1.

Same Shade Cases: 3/cg: The remaining cases, including "3/cg", all have the two White knights starting on the same shade of square as each other (**D**). Thus no Black knight starts on the same color as any White knight. Before their first move, the White and Black knights pressure different shade squares. After a White and Black knight each hop forward once, they again pressure different shade squares. Thus neither prevents the other from advancing to rank 5: they seem as unable to interact as two enemy bishops of opposite shades.

Hypermodern or Pawn Occupancy

Does a given setup weigh in favor of occupying the center with pawns, or in favor of a more remote or hypermodern control of the center?

This attribute is greatly affected by Bishop placement. It might also be influenced by rook placement. Consider the symmetrical setup R#347-S#329 NRQB-BKRN. No bishop is in good position to strike the center from a safe distance away, in hypermodern fashion. Folly for White would be **1. e23 Nh8g6 2.**

Bd1f3 Ng6e5. Starting from the corners the two knights can exert only half the pressure on the four center squares as chess1 players take for granted from their knights. Controlling the center from afar with pieces seems implausible in R#347.

In contrast, the setup R#078-S#295 QNBR-KRNB would support hypermodern play well. We could see early White moves of b23 Bc1b2 g23. Players would likely open with e24 or d24 less frequently than they do in chess1, favoring the immediate activation of covered diagonal pressure through the center.

Predictions

The history of science overwhelmingly shows that incorrect theories often, or even usually have a beneficial effect on the advancement of that science. We need engines that produce testable hypotheses. A hypothesis provides a structure for deeper inquiry. When organized tests are conducted generating results that reject a hypothesis and disprove at least part of the theory, we are left with new organized information we did not have before the test. Often new truths are gleaned from the test data, leading to better theories, and the cycle continues. It is in this spirit that I will now make a few modest predictions about the early course of chess960 games, based on their setup attributes. I would rather be clearly wrong than be less wrong through vagueness or risk avoidance.

1. **Bishop separation:** When White's bishops are setup with two squares between them, and the queen occupies one of those squares, the opening phase will see relatively fewer pawn moves. R#913-S#829 RKNB-QRBN is one example we have data for, from Mainz 2005/08 round 3. R#362 from chess1 is another example.

2. **Corner queens:** Most corner queens will make their first move diagonally.

3. **Corner bishop pair and castling:** In setups with an adjacent bishop pair in the 'a' corner, 'a' wing castling will be rare. The reason is the inevitably poor pawn presence for a king fort on such an 'a' wing. Again, the pair Bg1 and Bh1 is a reciprocal situation that would follow the same prediction. An example would be R#023-S#783 QRKN-RNBB (played in Mainz 2003/08 round 4).

4. **Four corner bishops and hypermodern strategies:** The hypermodern approach to central control will be chosen more frequently in setups with all four corners occupied by bishops. However, this propensity favoring hypermodernism will be less pronounced when the four corners are occupied by one bishop and one queen of each color. An example would be R#716-S#643 BRNK-RQNB (played in Mainz 2003/08 round 1). The corner queens will have to be protected from the enemy bishops by the interposition of center pawns.

5. **Penetration by unopposed knights:** Knights will cross into enemy territory (meaning beyond their rank 4) earlier in setups with no knight opposition. An example would be R#112-S#001 BQNB-NRKR (played in Mainz 2004/08 round 6).

Some of these predictions are put to the test in the next chapter. However, my primary intent with the setup attributes system is to bring some order to perceived chaos. The system makes simple recommendations that beginning chess960 players may not properly emphasize on their own. The predictions I have offered are another way of looking at those recommendations.

8

From Setup Attributes to Opening Moves

In this chapter we turn our attention to actual chess960 games played by masters attending the annual Mainz event each August. In Mainz, all games within any one round use the same randomly chosen initial setup. We will focus on one setup at a time, gathering together several games that all used that same setup. We will catalog the attributes of the setup, and use those attributes to give advice or make predictions about the opening play. Then we will see how well those predictions matched the realities of several games that used the setup.

How Much Variability?: We are generally interested in commonalities shared among games within each setup. The ability of any system to make predictions about opening play is strongest when the opening play is relatively unvaried. So we will watch for any kind of sameness among games starting from the same setup. We will watch for different players making the same mobilization maneuvers, or creating the same pawn structures, or coordinating their pieces in the same way, or conducting attacks on the same wing in some similar way or under similar conditions, and so on.

In the chess1 world the openings are studied in the mode of specific variations. For chess960 we need an alternative approach. The opening phase is more complex in chess960 than in chess1. One of my goals in this book is to show how a system of opening study in chess960 might look or might be developed, and to show how different it would be from the hard calculation approach possible in static chess1. I am not making any grand claims for my system. My system introduces a new approach for bringing some comprehensible order to chess960 setups that otherwise can make a player feel disoriented in the opening phase.

Most of the opening ideas are discussed from White's perspective, but of course most apply equally well to Black.

The two diagrams below show the first two initial setups examined in the sections that follow. Note especially that both contain adjacent bishops.

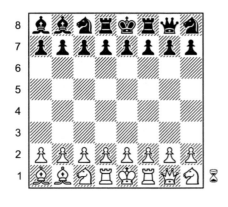

R#731

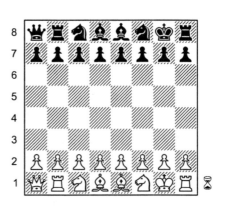

R#155

R#731 - S#352 BBNR-KRQN

Game/20 minutes, 5 seconds delay
Mainz, Germany, chess960 "FiNet" Open
2003/08, Round 2

Cataloging:

Here is my cataloging of R#731 setup attributes.

Undefended rank 2 pawns.	None. Pa2 potential vulnerability from Qg8 may irritate by tying down Bb1.
Undefended rank 4 squares.	White cannot easily defend the rank 4 squares a-c,h. White has motive to advance c24 and f24.
Corner piece mobilization plans.	Black should open with b76. Unpleasant for Black might be 1. g23 c75 2. Qg12 c76 blocking Ba8. Nh1g3 will be desired. White must decide promptly whether he wants an advanced pawn presence on this 'h' wing. See king fort. Perhaps White may redeploy his adjacent Ba1 Bb1 by plies a23 b24 Bb1a2. This Ba2 would strike more deeply into enemy territory than Bb1. It would harass heavy enemy pieces, and it is defended by Nc1.
King fort.	The adjacent corner bishops Ba1 Bb1 recommend 'h' wing castling. The idea of 'h' side castling is scary due to the raking pressure from enemy Ba8 Bb8.

	This setup is more inviting of the hypermodern approach to central control, so it might be plausible to establish an enduring king fort in the center columns and not castle. Neither 'a' nor 'h' side castling seems inviting in this setup.
Is there knight opposition?	Full. There is potential for unopposed knight penetration by Nh1g3 Ng3h5, to coordinate pressure with Ba1 on square g7.
Hypermodern or central pawn advance?	There is some support for hypermodern in this setup, but neither Bb1 nor Qg1 press either of the two rank 5 central squares (d5 and e5). With Ba1 Rd1 Qg1, a pawn advance of 1. d24 would be superbly supported.

From the above cataloging I would make the following predictions.

Specific Predictions:

1. This setup contains much diagonal pressure emanating from the corner areas, able to reach enemy rank 2 pawns (once their pressure is discovered). Yet there are no undefended rank 2 pawns on either wing. Thus Black should not have to waste any early tempos fending off a White initiative in the earliest moves.

2. White wants to develop by discovery his two bishops. That must include c24. Since square c4 is undefended by White, and since the Pb2 must also advance, I would expect a very early b23 followed by c24.

3. The bishops might not move until the middle game.

4. Black will open with b76 if White opens g23.

5. White will likely play Nh1g3 without first playing g24. This will preserve the option of 'h' wing castling, even if that option is not used.

6. White will not advance both his 'f' and his central pawns to rank 4. That would leave his king too exposed regardless of whether the king is kept in the center or in either wing.

7. Minimal knight penetrations are expected. Any that do occur will likely lead to immediate exchanges.

Opening Moves Tables and Diagrams for R#731:

The plies of each game run down its column. The games are sorted left-to-right by the origin square then destination square of their plies (example, square a8 sorts just prior to b1). Any italicized plies are duplicates of those to their left. This arrangement highlights some kinds of sameness between games. Only the first 12 plairs are shown, as this chapter is focused on the opening phase.

The rest of the moves are in PGN files downloadable from ChessTigers.de. However, some PGN files created before 2005/08 have castling related flaws that must be hand-corrected (not hard to do) before Arena or Fritz9 will replay them smoothly. The 2005 release of Shredder Classic is unable to comprehend the PGN files created before 2005/08, and is also unable to comprehend the backward compatible 2005/08 PGN files. So Chess Tigers created a second set of PGN files that use Shredder-FEN notation, just to support Shredder.

Chess Tigers is able to publish only a subset of its chess960 games because they rely on electronic DGT boards to track the rapid games. This equipment is expensive, so most games are played without. Spurred on by Chess Tigers, DGT enabled its handy sensor-board software for full chess960 support in time for the 2005/08 tournament.

White's d-e Pawns Unmoved: The R#731 diagrams that follow show the end-of-opening position for each game in the moves table. They provide another way to display and detect sameness. For instance, one sameness is that among all those diagrams White rarely advanced either of his two central column pawns. This pawn structure element is very rare in chess1, yet in R#731 we see it occur consistently. Together these observations tell us two things.

First, the opening principles of chess and chess1 are indeed different, just as theorized earlier in this book. As John Watson emphasized, proper play is derived from the particulars of the position, not from general principles. Setups are positions. We are seeing that the styles of opening play are based on the setup position. Our understanding of chess opening principles has been misled by our exclusive usage of R#362.

Second, the R#731 game data is delightfully strong evidence that there are interesting styles of logical chess play that we see occasionally in chess960 but only rarely in chess1. The consistency of play between these grandmasters proves their play is not weird or unnatural for chess (they had not consulted each other before or during these R#731 games). It is time for us to stop missing out on these other equally valid and interesting alternative styles, both as players and as spectators.

After the R#731 diagrams, a summary of each game is given. For each game, the reader should replay the moves on a board first, then read the summary for that game.

Plair	DB-RK	AD-IF	FVP-AP	LN-VM
1	b24	c24	*c24*	*c24*
	d75	b76	c75	e76
2	Nc1b3	b23	b23	f24
	Nc8d6	f76	e75	f75
3	Nh1g3	Nh1g3	f24	Nh1g3
	Ke8c/Rd	Qg8f7	b76	b76
4	a24	f24	f4:e5	b23
	Rf8e	Nh8g6	Nh8g6	c75
5	f24	Qg1f2	Nc1d3	Ng3h5
	f76	Ke8g/Rf	d75	Rf87
6	f45	f45	c4:d5	g24
	e75	Ng6e5	Ba8:d5	Nh8g6
7	f5:e6/e5	Ba1:Ne5	Nh1g3	g4:f5
	Qg8:e6	f6:Be5	Nc8e7	e6:f5
8	Nb3c5	Ke1g/Rf	Rd1c	d24
	Qe67	c75	Ne7c6	Bb8d6
9	Qg1d4	Bb1e4	Qg1e3	d45
	Nd6e4	d75	Ke8c/Rd	Nce7
10	Ng3:Ne4	c4:d5	b34	Nc1d3
	d5:Ne4	Ba8:d5	Rf8e	Ke8c/Rd
11	Qd4e3	Nc1d3	b4:c5	Ke1c/Rd
	Rd86	e76	b65	Rd8e
12	Rf14	Qf2e3	Ng3f5	Nd3e5
	b75	Bd5:Be4	Ng6:e5	Rf78

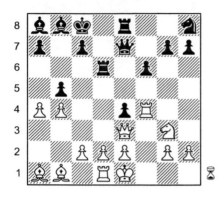

D.Baramidze – R.Kazimdzhanov
After 12. Rf14 b75.

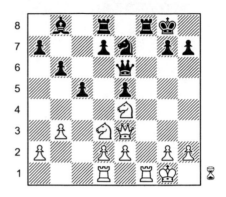

A.Dreev – I.Farago
After 12. Qf2e3 Bd5:Be4 13. f5:e6 Qf7:e6
14. Ng3:Be4 Nc8e7.

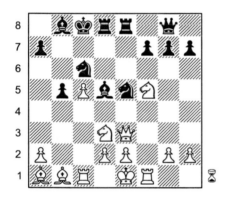

F.Vallejo Pons – A.Petrosian
After 12. Ng3f5 Ng6:e5.

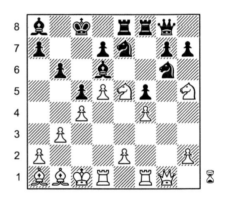

L.Nisipeanu – V.Meijers
After 12. Nd3e5 Rf78.

A.Dreev - I.Farago, R#731, 1-0:

White went hypermodern in the opening and won in the endgame. After the opening White had not advanced either central pawn. Indeed both of White's central pawns were on their original squares blocked by his own pieces! It was not until the 45th ply of the game that White finally moved a central pawn, and then only to rank 3. However, as the opening ended (the first 12 plairs), both of White's bishops were gone. Thus it would seem White did not gain much control over the center.

Both players castled 'h' wing early even though the setup had both enemy bishops firing at the king fort. Black castled before any bishops had left the game. Only Black matched my prediction of a one rank advance of the 'f' pawn. Aside from the 'f' pawns, the king fort pawns in columns g-h were not advanced until ply 44, by which time the endgame had arrived.

As predicted there was little knight penetration, even later in the game. However, the knight opposition arrangement seems not to have been the reason.

F.Vallejo Pons - A.Petrosian, R#731, 1-0:

White again went hypermodern and emerged from the opening with an advantage. This may have been due to Black being too clever with his third ply (3... e5:f4 would have been safer). Black castled into a highly exposed 'a' wing. White was able to take his time castling because his unmoved center pawns provided protection. On his ply 18 White castled 'h' wing enjoying the cover of his unmoved pawns in g-h. Black was hindered by the long delayed activity of his nearly cornered queen. The paucity of advanced centered pawns made knight penetrations awkward. With so many pieces overlapping pressure in the four center squares, all without pawn obstruction, conditions were ripe for a flurry of piece exchanges. Later plairs 13-18 saw eight pieces leave the game, including the queens. White emerged ahead by the exchange (of minor piece for rook).

L.Nisipeanu - V.Meijers, R#731, 1-0:

As in the other games that began 1. c24, White played an early f24, in a Benoni-like pincer attack on the enemy's center advances. I see little purpose to Black's tempo wasting 1... e76. It left Black with no counter-attack options and only an awkward defense when White penetrated with 5. Ng3h5 to coordinate pressure on g7. This maneuver becomes well known to chess960 players. After the opening 12 plairs an interesting position was established, rather unlike anything seen in chess1. Both players castled toward their corner adjacent bishop pair, and so had minimal pawn coverage for their king forts. The center was closed by White's 9. d45 which made the kings safer than they at first appeared when they were subsequently castled. After Black's 19... Rf8:Qg the position looked normal for a chess1 game.

D.Baramidze - R.Kazimdzhanov, R#731, 1-0:

Both players delayed activating their cornered adjacent bishop pair, and each seemed to be hurt by the delay. White could have captured Black's Pe4 were it not for the obstruction of White's Bb1 by Pc2. Black's king fort was non-existent after he had to sacrifice his Pc7 to activate Bb8. With essentially no 'a' wing pawns for Black, White was able to strongly post his Nc5 in front of the vulnerable enemy Kc8.

Summary of All R#731 Games:

Bigger Advantage for White?: White won all four games. Perhaps this setup is one that prompts the Mainz grandmasters to say some chess960 setups give White an even bigger advantage than they get in the chess1 setup R#362-S#518. The FFM (Fair First Move) rule proposal may be especially desirable in this setup. However, I tallied data for the chess1 rounds played in Mainz, and I found that some of those rounds also had lopsided win rates for White. White's dominance in those particular rounds is due to the imperfect laws of probability and to natural variation. So the results of this chess960 round cannot be taken as strong evidence R#731 gives White an advantage larger than average. We take a more thorough and rigorous study of win-loss data per color in a later chapter.

The overriding attribute of this setup is its cornered adjacent bishop pair on the 'a' wing. With R#731 White usually played a hypermodern approach to the center, and adhered to it in the extreme, even blocking his Pd2 and Pe2. The repeated use of 1. c24 to open put pawn pressure on the four center squares without occupying any of them with a pawn. Black responded by advancing his center pawns, though White advanced f24 to counter this. This desire to counter the enemy pawn presence in the center may be why my prediction of f23 proved incorrect. With White holding back both of his center pawns, the 'f' pawn was needed to challenge the enemy's center.

This R#731 setup is exceptionally interesting in the castling dilemma it sets for each player. Contrary to my prediction, the king forts were often established on the 'a' wing containing the adjacent bishop pair. Consequently the king forts were often of atrocious quality. Perhaps players decided a good king fort under attack by the enemy bishop pair was less safe than a poor king fort elsewhere. I was wrong in predicting White would move f23 for added king fort safety, as instead they played f24 for stronger center control.

My prediction of relatively few bishop moves during the opening was partially accurate. Among the 100 plies shown in the opening table, only two were bishop moves not involving a capture. There were only six bishop moves overall.

Advances of the 'g' pawns were rare, as predicted. The 'h' corner knights preferred developing to rank 3 rather than rank

2, as predicted. We did see the maneuver Nh1g3 Ng3h5 to coordinate pressure on square g7.

It is hard to draw firm conclusions about my prediction of minimal knight penetrations across the frontier line.

Overall I feel that R#731 is an exceptionally interesting setup. It gives players the option to conduct a style of opening play we rarely get to see in chess1. I find the R#731 castling dilemma fascinating. In the June 2004 edition of *Chess Life*, WCC Vladimir Kramnik explained his feeling that FRC would be better if the setups having a bishop in a corner were eliminated. If Kramnik meant to include R#731 among those he would eliminate, then I do not share his feeling. Kramnik does make an important observation that there is only one way to develop a corner bishop, and that this seems constraining. It is ironic to hear a concern that chess960 sometimes lacks variety.

R#155 - S#393 QRNB-BNKR

Game/20 minutes, 5 seconds delay
Mainz, Germany, chess960 "FiNet Open"
2003/08/14, Round 3

The R#155 setup we now examine is very different from R#731. Here the bishops are still adjacent but they occupy the two center squares.

Cataloging:
Here is my cataloging of setup R#155 attributes.

Undefended rank 2 pawns.	None.

Undefended rank 4 squares.	White cannot easily defend the rank 4 squares c,e-f with pieces. White has flexibility over whether to advance his c-f pawns to rank 4 to liberate his bishops Bd1 Be1.
Corner piece mobilization plans.	The 'b' pawns will have to advance to activate the 'a' corner queens. White's Rh1 might not participate in castling. Instead it might be activated along the 'h' column by h24 h45 advancement. This might coordinate with Qa1 in an attack on the Black king situated on the 'h' wing.
King fort.	No pieces need to be cleared away from rank 1 to get the king safely into the 'h' corner. The 'h' wing pawns do not have to be advanced in order to liberate the queen and bishops. The king is already in a safe corner. That removes one of the two common motivations for castling. Players might forego castling and use the 'h' pawn for attack.
Is there knight opposition?	Partial/Low. The knights have unopposed access to rank 5 in the two mid-board columns e,f.
Hypermodern or central pawn advance?	There is little piece support directed to the center rank 4 squares. Nor can the knights protect those squares after one move (unless they hop away from the center of the board to near the edge, unpleasant).

149

> Nor is there enough piece placement to support a hypermodern center.

From the above cataloging I would make the following predictions.

Specific Predictions:

- There are reasons to predict moves f23 e24 Be1f2 d24. This fights for the four center squares in a manner that builds the necessary support for Pd4 Pe4. It opens lines for both bishops. It avoids blocking the Qa1 as would the reciprocal moves c23 d24 Bd1c2 e24. And it clears central column space for the knights to develop to without blocking central pawns stuck on rank 2.

- All signs point to 'h' wing castling. Or we might see the voluntary foregoing of castling accompanied by h24 h45 to activate the Rh1 for attack.

- There is the threat of unopposed enemy knights having easy penetration to rank 5 center squares. I would predict players will use their c-f pawns positioned on rank 3 to keep these knights away.

Opening Moves Tables and Diagrams for R#155:

Plair	AY-LN	IS-IG	CB-AD	AH-FVP
1	d24	e24	e24	Nf1g3
	d75	e75	Nf8e6	e75
2	Nc1d3	b24	Nf1e3	e23
	Nf8g6	d76	b75	d75

3	b23 Nc8d6	d24 e5:d4	d23 Nc8b6	b23 Nf8g6
4	e23 e76	Qa1:d4 Nf8e6	Nc1e2 d75	Nc1d3 f76
5	Nf1g3 a75	Qd43 Kg8/Rhf	e4:d5 Nb6:d5	c24 Be8f7
6	a24 b76	Nc1e2 b75	Be1d2 c75	c4:d5 Bf7:d5
7	f24 Ng6h4	Nf1e3 Nc8b6	Ne3:Nd5 Qa8:Nd5	Nd3b4 Bd5f7
8	Kg1/Rhf Kg8/Rhf	c23 Be8c6	Ne2c3 Qd5b7	d24 e5:d4
9	Bd1e2 f76	Bd1c2 Rf8e	Bd1f3 Be8c6	Qa1:d4 Kg8/Rhf
10	Be1f2 Be8g6	f23 Nb6c4	Bf3:Bc6 Qb7:Bc6	Ng3f5 Nc8e7
11	Rb1e Nh4f5	Be1f2 Bd8g5	Rb1e Kg8/Rhf	Nf5g3 c76
12	Ng3:Nf5 Bg6:Nf5	Ne3:Nc4 b5:Nc4	Qa1d Ne6d4	Nb4d3 Bd8b6

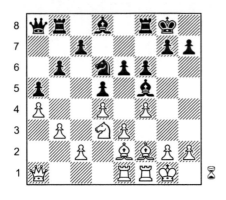

A.Yusupov – L.Nisipeanu
After 12. Ng3:Nf5 Bg6:Nf5.

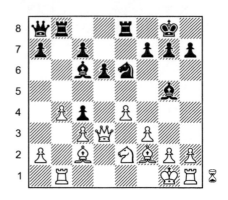

I.Sokolov – I.Glek
After 12. Ne3:Nc4 b5:Nc4.

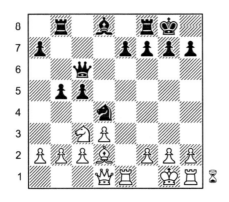

C.Bauer – A.Dreev
After 12. Qa1d Ne6d4.

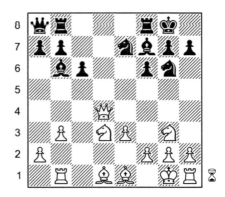

A.Huzman – F.Vallejo Pons
After 12. Nb4d3 Bd8b6.

A.Yusupov - L.Nisipeanu, R#155, .5-.5:

The White and Black pawn structures in this game were relatively symmetrical. Both players made early advances of their two center pawns. These pawn advances pressured the center and opened lines for both light and dark bishops. Both of the 'b' pawns made early advances also, to free their queens.

Both players castled 'h' side with strong king forts. Shortly thereafter the 'f' pawns were advanced to open a diagonal for the bishops. After the first six plairs all four knights had been developed. Even though the knight opposition rating was low, the knights were unable to penetrate across the frontier line. The position was perfectly symmetrical between White and Black after the first six plairs. This went on to be a lively chess game despite the fact it ended in a draw.

After the opening, White's ply 13 was g24, leaving only his 'h' pawn in place from his original king fort. White had a lot of free space behind his 'h' wing pawns.

Black found an entertaining way to solve his cornered queen mobilization problem, zigzagging it along perpendicular diagonals to shift it to the opposite wing, and on to loop around the board. Qa8-c6-e8-g6-h5-f3-f4-g5-f5-b1-b3.

I.Sokolov – I.Glek, R#155, 0-1:

Early in the game White moved 4. Qa1:d4, and Black naturally replied with tempo by 4... Nf8e6 5. Qd43. White did in a sense lose a tempo here, but he also redeployed his queen from a corner to a central column. White could argue this queen maneuver was valuable and did not lose a tempo. We can also imagine in another setup that the knights could start on columns c,g instead of c,f. In that case White's Qa1 could move to the central d4 square without immediate risk of being run off by an enemy knight. In chess1 all of the knights are easily placed on squares from which they saturate the four center squares with pressure, but this is not so in most other setups. Thus most setups may have a bit more freedom to violate Nimzovich's opening principle against early queen development.

Black did penetrate with 10... Nb6c4, but 12. Ne3:Nc4 soon followed. My prediction was for 'c' or 'f' pawns to be positioned on rank 3 to prevent knight penetrations. White played both c23 and f23, though Black played neither equivalent. In this game square d6 was occupied by a pawn. Black played to control square d5 for a freeing pawn advance, but then chose Nb6c4 instead of d65. The knight opposition level was low, but it is in terms of preventing penetration onto one of the four center squares. There is no surprise then that White was able to immediately exchange off Black's knight that penetrated to c4.

White's pawn moves did include the predicted f23 e24 d24, though not in that sequence.

C.Bauer – A.Dreev, R#155, .5-.5:

With 1... Nf8e6 Black gives a hint that c75 may soon follow, which it did in plair 6. Black activated his Qa8 diagonally, whereas White waited until the horizontal Qa1d was possible. After 7... Qa8:Nd5 Black probably lost a tempo by 8. Ne2c3 Qd5b7.

The two 'h' wing king forts were pawn perfect. As the game progressed into the middle game neither player's position featured any major weaknesses.

Black was able to penetrate with a knight to square d4.

Summary of All R#155 Games:

Overall there were fewer early pawn advances than are seen in many other setups. Also, the pawn advances tended to look like traditional pawn advances in chess1, in that they were in the central columns and the 'h' wing king fort pawns were left in place. These factors probably caused R#155 to have a much higher draw rate than did R#731, 22% v. 10% respectively (among all games that round between titled players, not just the few published in PGN format).

An early advance of the 'b' pawn was seen in 5 of 8 cases. The queen was moved in the opening in 4 of 8 cases, all but one of them having its first move be diagonal. Further, every diagonal first move of a queen was to take a piece. Often these queens were promptly attacked, but not in all cases did that result in the queen costing a lost tempo, as she needed to be deployed from the corner anyway. In the four R#731 games, the rate of cornered 'a' column bishop moves during the opening was only 3 of 8, though again those first moves were to take a piece.

R#155 has knights on columns c,f which rates as partial/low knight opposition. Knight penetration was minimal in these four games. The knights started in columns c,f forcing a decision about whether to consider knights on d3 and e3 (and d6 and e6) well centered or well positioned. In no case did any player develop both his knights so as to occupy these two squares.

Castling was always to the 'h' wing.

Setup Attributes Assessed for Chess1

R#362 - S#518 RNBQ-KBNR (chess1)

Game/20 minutes, 5 seconds delay
Mainz, Germany, chess1 "Ordix Open"
2003/08 (all rounds)

Now we consider the well known R#362 setup position of chess1. We might presume the chess1 setup is less amenable to our approach of setup attribute analysis than are other chess960 setups. The reason is that attribute analysis cannot give as good and comprehensive knowledge about how to play the opening phase as can decades of analysis of this one setup. Large databases honed by trial and error may overwhelm any value we can derive from attribute analysis. Nevertheless it might be interesting to catalog the attributes for R#362. The primary claim being made for attribute analysis is that it is better than every other proposal so far published about how to handle a random chess960 opening: in other words, setup attribute analysis is better than nothing.

Cataloging:

Here is my cataloging of setup R#362 attributes.

Undefended rank 2 pawns.	None.
Undefended rank 4 squares.	b4 and e4. However, White has no motive for an early b24, and the square e4 is easy to defend with Nb1c3.
Corner piece mobilization plans.	The two corner rooks will very likely move along row 1 toward a more central column.
	Castling will be the likely mode for activating one of the corner rooks. The Rh1 may be used for castling more often than the Ra1, simply because there are fewer pieces between the Rh1 and the Ke1.
King fort.	No wing pawns must be moved in order to clear the way for castling.

	No wing pawns need be moved in order to activate the non-castling pieces. However, b23 or g23 might be desired to improve bishop activation via fianchetto to the long diagonal. Fianchetto would maintain the bishop at a safe distance from enemy knights. By avoiding moves like Bf1d3 and Bc1e3, fianchetto would also keep unobstructed any rank 1 queen or rooks that can press along the two central columns.
Is there knight opposition?	Full. Any knight seeking to invade into enemy territory through the center will be subject to immediate exchange by an enemy knight. Knights begin on the squares that give them perfect access to pressure the center. Knights might be able to penetrate along the wings (such as Ng1f3g5).
Hypermodern or central pawn advance?	Fianchetto is the only way a hypermodern attack on the center can be mounted. Fianchetto is tempo consuming, and it can weaken the pawns for a king fort.

From the above cataloging I would make the following predictions.

Specific Predictions:

1. The majority of games will open with 1. e24 or 1. d24, due to the mediocre opportunities for hypermodern play.

2. The ratio of 'h' side castling to 'a' side castling will be about 3/2. This is because there are 3 pieces to clear away for 'a' side castling but only 2 for 'h' side.

3. Most attempts at hypermodern play will involve the bishop that can fianchetto away from the castling wing. Thus most fianchetto maneuvers will be Bc1b2.

4. When 'a' side castling occurs, that player will likely advance his 'f' pawn by or before the early middle game. Similarly, for 'h' side castling we expect an early advance of pawn 'c'.

5. Both knights will usually make the initial move that presses on two of the four prized center squares, meaning Nb1c3 and Ng1f3.

6. King forts may often enjoy the high quality of three undisturbed wing pawns. However, attacks against such king forts may have success due to an inability of a cramped defender to obtain open lines for transferring his pieces to that wing for defense.

I know that predictions #2 and #3 are wrong. But if R#362 had been like any regular chess960 setup and never deeply analyzed, they are predictions I would have made using attribute analysis. This may put into sobering perspective the level of trust deserved by any predictions made for other chess960 setups based on analyses of their attributes.

I own a lot of chess1 books. Several make the same general comment about castling 'a' wing, saying the spacious 'a' wing gives the enemy more opportunities to attack the king. I vaguely understand this just from playing chess, but objectively I see three columns on each wing. The Qd1 is an extra piece that must be moved before 'a' wing castling, but the rate of 'a' wing castling is drastically less than for 'h' wing, seemingly more than the Qd1 can account for. A likely contributing factor is that the asymmetry in the castling rule leaves the castled Kc1 too close to the central columns to be considered tucked safely in the corner, and a precious tempo must be spent to get the king to column 'b'. The castled rook Rd1 does not later require a tempo to reach the important center the way Rf1e is often necessary after 'h' wing castling. However this seems to be inadequate compensation.

9

Is the Middle Game
Really the Same?

Chess960 is just chess, even though it may not look like chess the first time you see a randomly chosen setup. I am never surprised to read quotations like this:

> "It feels like normal chess. But there is no theory yet." *(Vishy Anand 2003, speaking about chess960 and R#272-S#017 BNQB-NRKR in particular,* ChessTigers.de.*)*

There is a general consensus that somehow games of chess960 turn into games of chess1 at about the start of the middle game:

> "About 10-15 moves were needed to reach positions reminiscent of classical chess." *(Erne Hirman 1996, as reported in Gligoric's* Shall We Play Fischerandom Chess?*)*

> "Usually we get a normal position after around 10-15 moves, but sometimes we forget to develop some pieces, because they are on odd squares." *(Peter Svidler 2002, from* ChessTigers.de*)*

I agree with a carefully qualified interpretation of the 10-15 plair view expressed in those two quotations. Yet we need to dig deeper into this subject before we can truly understand the relationships between chess960 and chess1 in terms of the middle game.

Awkward Middle Game Positions?

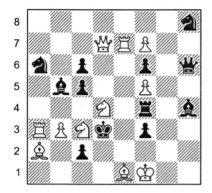

Diagram mga_10.

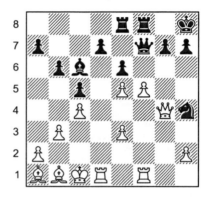

Diagram mga_11.

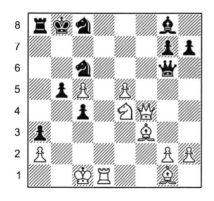

Diagram mga_12.

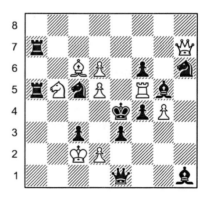

Diagram mga_13.

Does chess960 lead to awkward middle game positions? Here are four middle game position diagrams. Can you determine which two came from live chess960 play?

I think it will be easy for most readers to determine which positions came from real chess play versus which are composed problems or puzzles (very slightly tweaked so there may be no solution). We do not have formulas that tell us the answer, but our human intuition digests these complex visuals with seeming ease. The two composed puzzle positions have their own purposes and in their own way they are very interesting. These chess puzzles can be reached by legal chess1 or chess960 play. However their kind of middle game positions rarely or never occur in any real play. Compared to live chess play they would be considered random, chaotic, awkward, and artificial.

My point here is that chess960 middle game positions could not be accurately described by any of those negative adjectives (chaotic, artificial etc). Chess960 middle game positions have a normalcy about them, as is demonstrated by how sharply they contrast with the artificial positions. You were able to pick them out from the group as easily as if they had arisen from chess1. These chess960 positions arose from logical play, and thus they have intelligent structure and patterns in them no less than do chess1 positions. If they still feel some how odd it is only because chess1 is such a severe subset of Caissa's chess. Some of the structures that can in theory arise in fundamental chess are unreachable from chess1.

The Urge to Merge

In the comparisons between chess960 versus chess1, the general consensus is that they differ a lot in the opening phase, they merge very early during the middle game phase, and they are identical during the whole endgame phase. There is no doubt about the opening phase differences. The endgame phase will be addressed in a later chapter. The concern of this chapter is to look closely at the merge that supposedly happens very early in the middle game phase.

An eventual merge seems inevitable. Any chess960 setup will retain its individual character to an ever decreasing degree as additional moves are played. The merge does not happen because games from two different setups eventually reach similar positions. Rather the merge occurs when each game has lost its clues to its initial position, if that is the criterion we choose to use. The merge concept applies to the comparison of any two chess960 setups. But I will mostly speak in terms of a merge between the R#362 of chess1 and some imaginary average chess960 setup.

A major question concerns the number of plairs at which the two games typically merge. As we shall see, the answer depends on how we more precisely define the term 'merge' in this context. Even assessing the rate of the merge turns out to be an exercise in defining the term 'merge'. In terms of the internal feeling one gets from playing chess960 versus chess1, the two games merge before the end of the opening. But by a rigorous definition of 'merge', I believe chess960 and chess1 do not merge until the second half of the middle game. The loose consensus that has put the merge point earlier in the game, near say White's 13th move, seems to be an informal compromise between these two extremes.

I will make another major point right now. Nobody should want the merge to happen early in the ply count. We do not need a duplicate of chess1, rather we want to experience the full expanse of chess. We need a later merge in order to have that rich variety of experience.

Next we consider alternative definitions for the term 'merge' in our context. Further below we will put these definitions to the test.

Merge By Becoming Indistinguishable

One useful definition of 'merge' is captured by the concept of whether the positions from the two rule sets are distinguishable. At the extreme of an endgame position of K+P v. K there probably is no way to make any educated guess about whether the game is chess960 or chess1, no way to be any more reliable than a coin flip. As we work backward from endgame to middle game, we replace ever more pieces back onto the board. We could accumulate several pieces on the board and still not be able to say with confidence whether the game is chess960. As we continue working backward and get ever nearer to the opening, the position will eventually show a piece too oddly placed for chess1.

As one example, in chess1 games I have seen thousands of bishops fianchettoed as Bg2 or Bg7. I have seen this same g76 Bf8g7 maneuver repeatedly over and over, to point of being tired of it (as was Rudolf Spielmann in 1928). But in chess1 I have never seen a queen fianchettoed. When the majority of pieces are on the board and I see a queen fianchettoed Qg2 or Qg7, I immediately suspect chess960, even if every other piece on the crowded board occupies a familiar square. In chess1 each piece has its own set or range of familiar squares, which is unfortunate when you think about how narrow and repetitive that is. When the board is crowded, seeing something as innocent as a White Nd3 or Ne3 raises suspicions the game is not chess1 and is not setup R#362-S#518 from chess960. Even seeing something as supposedly normal as Black castled on the 'a' wing raises a hint of suspicion. These show how genuine are the inherent limitations against variety in chess1. There are many other examples I could site, especially where small groupings of 2-3 pieces are concerned. Most of these piece placements or groupings are legal and possible in chess1, but we all intuitively know they occur rarely or never. These odd placements and groupings usually make it easy to distinguish which of two chess positions came from chess960 versus chess1. A couple of oddly placed pieces may create a pattern outside the set of patterns grandmasters are said to have absorbed. Yet from my experience, I say with confidence that a couple of oddly placed pieces cannot prevent the pervasive overall perception that the position as a whole feels proper for chess, and as proper as any chess1 position.

In most cases I see the rareness of these odd-for-chess1 piece placements and groupings as a regrettable deprivation for the chess1 world. Players who vow exclusivity to chess1 cannot seriously be thinking that maneuvers and placements like Bf1g2, Bc1g5, Qd1c2, Ng1f3, and Nf3e5 are good for chess, but that it just so happens that all the other maneuvers inherent in the other 959 setups are bad for chess. Are those people opposed to chess960 claiming the style of king forts repetitiously seen in chess1 are good for chess, but that all the other kinds from the other 959 setups would be bad for chess? The claim must instead be that either (A) additional variety would be bad, perhaps because it would make chess too complicated, or (B) additional variety is unbeneficial because there is already enough variety in chess1.

The forward progression of any chess960 game eventually brings a ply which dislodges the last oddly placed piece and makes the position visually indistinguishable from chess1. Many pieces may have been exchanged off by the time this happens.

Merge By Intuitive Feeling of Proper-ness

A second useful definition of 'merge' is captured by our intuitive perception of whether any given chess position intuitively feels proper and not artificial. A feeling of proper-ness arises surprisingly early in chess960 games. Proper-ness certainly arises earlier than does the visual sameness discussed above. Proper-ness usually arises while there are still pieces that would be considered oddly placed for chess1. This early feeling of proper-ness is in full force the from the very first time a player competes in a chess960 game. This trend does not have to grow slowly over the first several chess960 games one plays.

This intuitive feeling, of chess960 merging with chess1 by the late opening, is so strong and reliable that for me it briefly led to an unexpected emotional let down. On the first few occasions when I successfully cajoled a chess1 pal to play an informal game of chess960, I noticed by the late opening there was no longer anything special about the moment or the game. After the first 9 moves or so, we were just playing chess like we had any number of times before. The special feeling of chess960 fades before the opening ends. Chess960 is just chess.

Merge By Reachable-ness

A third definition of 'merge' is the point at which a chess960 game (non-R#362) progresses to a position that could be reached by a legal chess1 game. This is not a useful definition. Starting from R#857-S#533 RNBB-KQNR it requires exactly one plair to achieve a position that can be reached from chess1, namely 1. e23 e76. In chess1 this same position can be reached by **e23 Qd1f3 Bf1e2 Be2d1 Qf3e2 Qe2f1**. This is only a minor curiosity. I wonder what is the earliest ply at which a chess960 game (non-R#362) has reached a position that has occurred in a chess1 game (castling rights being part of a position).

Reality Coincides With the Ideal

An advocate might try to sell chess960 to the chess1 community by saying the two games merge in the range of 10-15 plairs. I am an advocate of both chess1 and chess960, yet I discourage talk of an early merge. I believe the claim is partly inaccurate. Chess960 is just chess, but it is not chess1. The positions do not fully merge so early. Also, I think the underlying perspective is backwards. We do not want the earliest possible merge. As an extreme to make the point, it would be awful if chess960 were unable to remain distinct from chess1 for only 3 plairs. Much more interesting would be a merge that slowly evolves stretching well into the middle game. The chess960 position will achieve what feels like chess normalcy long before the ply that fully completes the merge with chess1. This early normalcy is a strength of chess960, as is its delayed merge with chess1. The ideal chess960 setup leads to games that have the feeling of normal chess after only a small number of plairs, but that remain distinguishable from chess1 for as many plairs deep as possible. A chess player who plays only chess1 can legitimately reject chess960 for himself if he savors the pre-game calculation aspect of chess1. But that spirit would taste sour if extended into the middle game.

Opening setups in chess1 are maximally restricted, and the repetition of common opening plair patterns continues as an inevitable consequence of that. But chess middle games had better come in all rational shapes and sizes. For the sake of players and especially for spectators, the more rational middle game variety that occurs among the games of a tournament the better. The only caveat is that we do not want to see middle game positions that look and feel chaotic, like composed "mate in 2" or "mate in 3" puzzles, where there exists no signs of prior intelligent play leading up to the position.

Two Assertions

In this chapter I make two major assertions. First, I claim that by choosing from among the few chess960 games published from the Mainz tournaments I can find several that have positions deep into the middle game that are unlike chess1 middle game positions. I claim these chess960 positions can be distinguished from chess1 without additional clues beyond the positions themselves. It was not hard to find chess960 positions around ply 45 that could serve in this demonstration.

Second, I claim that even when I give up game selection control to a random process like dice, distinctive differences between the positions of chess1 and chess960 exist in the middle game, though they fade at an earlier ply count.

I am not claiming the diagram comparisons I offer in this chapter prove my assertions. These comparisons do give some support to my assertions, but the test case count is far too small to truly prove anything, and other experimental rigors would be needed as well. Mostly the comparisons are meant to provide a vivid demonstration of my two major assertions. Next, the comparison details are described.

Visualizing the Merge

As a game of chess960 progresses, it eventually reaches a position that looks normal for the chess1 rule set. This similarity appears even though the chess960 position may retain characteristics that make it distinguishable from chess1 on a probabilistic or statistical basis. Below are shown three sets of position diagrams. For the reader there are two primary tasks for each set. One, determine which diagrams came from chess1 and which came from chess960 (half in each set). Two, the reader should determine for himself whether all the positions feel proper for chess in general.

A. The 12 Plair End-of-Opening Boundary: The opening plair count of 10-15 has been offered as the approximate point at which chess1 and chess960 games merge. Since the opening-to-middle game boundary has been set historically at the first dozen plairs, this is a close enough match that we will adhere to exactly 12 plairs for all positions in this set.

The positions in these next four diagrams were chosen through quasi-random methods. I felt this comparison exercise demanded some non-random hand of sanity in choosing the positions to be shown. I felt it made sense to give less emphasis to the 960 different setups and more emphasis to the 480 reciprocal-pairs. Since 'a' side castling is uncommon in chess1, no 'a' side castled positions were allowed into these diagrams. Further, the only chess960 games eligible were ones where the king started in an 'h' wing column e-g. I required that each chess960 game start from a different initial setup (and no R#362 allowed).

On the chess1 side I required that each game start with a different opening (using three Sicilian Defense openings would skew the results). Even with different opening moves chess1 games have a tendency to cluster repetitively around similar early middle game positions or features. So I felt it necessary to discard some chess1 positions and search again until I found one that looked sufficiently different.

To make the comparisons as fair as possible, all games were chosen from the Mainz chess tournaments held each August. These large events host both a chess1 and a chess960 tournament in which the time controls are Game/20 minutes plus a 5 second delay. Only games involving two titled players were used. In most cases this meant GM v. GM, but IM and WFM etc were also eligible.

I believe these positions are easily categorized between chess1 and chess960. I believe that at the end of the opening phase (after plair 12), the games from the two rule sets will usually have yet to merge. See the four diagrams mgi_2* (answers are at the end of this book).

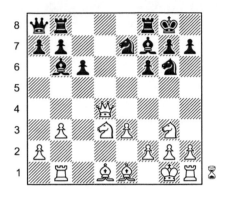

Diagram mgi_20.

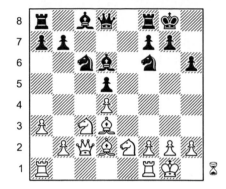

Diagram mgi_21.

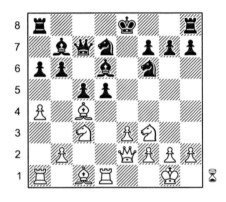

Diagram mgi_22.

Diagram mgi_23.

B. How Late Still Clearly Distinguishable?: The identification task will not be quite so easy for this next set of diagrams. For these next eight diagrams I tried to find games that were clearly distinguishable as late into the middle game as I could find. By clearly distinguishable I mean that most readers will feel confident they can identify the four chess960 games. In these diagrams there are still oddly placed pieces that provide clues to the original rule set, even though these clues are less blatant than in the earlier diagrams after 12 plairs.

Again the actual differences between chess1 and chess960 are bigger than I permitted my diagrams to show. I applied all the same restrictions as in the previous section (no 'a' side castling etc). My efforts yielded positions with an average ply count of 33, or plair 17. Examine diagrams mgb_3*.

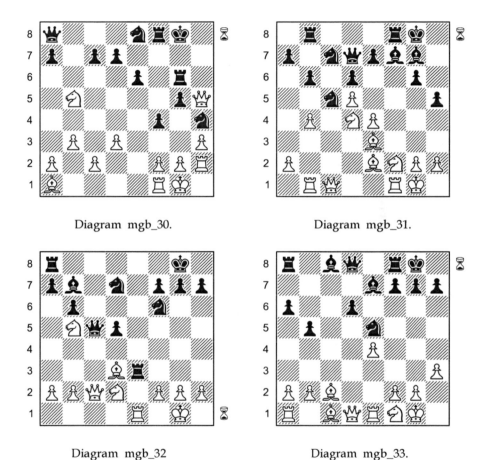

Diagram mgb_30.

Diagram mgb_31.

Diagram mgb_32

Diagram mgb_33.

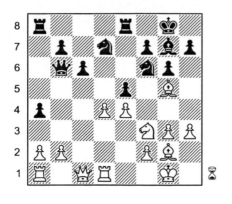

Diagram mgb_34.

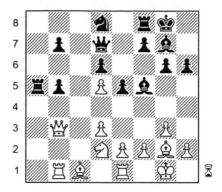

Diagram mgb_35.

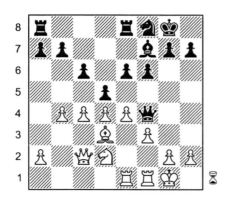

Diagram mgb_36.

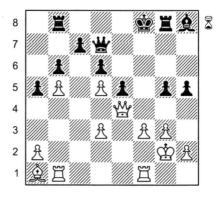

Diagram mgb_37.

C. Maximized Ply Counts: Next are the positions chosen to maximize the ply count while retaining distinctive characteristics rarely found in chess1 middle game positions. Half are from chess1. Which three are from chess960?

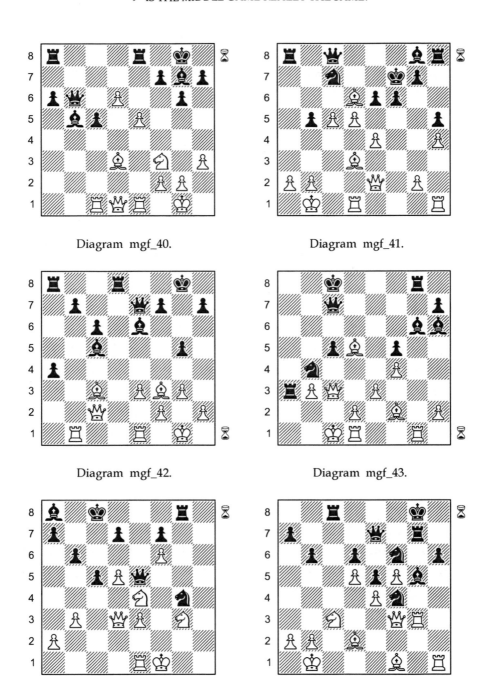

Diagram mgf_40.

Diagram mgf_41.

Diagram mgf_42.

Diagram mgf_43.

Diagram mgf_44.

Diagram mgf_45.

In the above positions, the average ply count reached 47, or plair 24. The chess960 clues in these diagrams are more subtle than in the previous section. I decided to partly lift the restriction against 'a' side castling for these next diagrams, to remind us that the true differences between the middle games of chess1 and chess960 are much larger than what my diagrams have been allowed to show. Examine diagrams mgf_4*.

I think most readers will be able to do better than pure chance or guesswork in categorizing the above diagrams, though many people might get one incorrect. If readers do believe they can categorize these diagrams more accurately than would a mechanism of pure chance, that means chess1 is narrowing the variety of middle game chess even more than most players have ever realized. Remember, the fresh patterns seen in chess960 arise from a long sequence of logical moves, which makes them very different from the kind of artificial pattern variety we see in chess puzzles. By identifying the chess960 positions the reader proves to himself that chess1 in practice does not include those position patterns in its repertoire. To me that shows chess1 represents a loss of chess wealth. However, to the tastes of some chess enthusiasts, chess1 makes up for this loss by being partly an at-home puzzle and thus only partly a sport. The chess960 patterns are uncommon in chess1, yet they still look normal for chess.

Svidler's Clarification: In a 2003 interview, Peter Svidler gave an opinion seemingly contradictory to one he expressed the following opinion about the middle game merge. From http://www.chessbase.com/ newsdetail.asp?newsid=1121, answering Harmut Metz, Svidler said (italics mine):

> "[In chess960], You see a few 'normal' positions in almost every game - but it can be a 'normal' *endgame* position by that time."

I understand Svidler to be saying that a full merge of chess1 and chess960 sometimes does not occur until the endgame is reached. I think the merge usually happens before the endgame, but I believe Svidler is right to shift the emphasis from the end of the opening to closer to the end of the middle game.

Comparisons Not Involving R#362: All this comparing between chess960 and chess1 tends to distract us from the many interesting comparisons that can be investigated between various setups of chess960 beyond R#362. At random we could pick any two chess960 setups and ask "When during a chess960 game of this setup does it become implausible to determine much about which of the 960 setups was used?" Aside from the castling aspect, I presume the answer, in plair counts, would vary widely based on the degree to which the two setups shared key attributes. I presume there are a few reciprocal-pairs that are different than R#362 + R#862 but which quickly lead to positions indistinguishable from it. In any case, each successive ply tends to create a position that looks plausible from ever more setups, until eventually all 480 reciprocal-pairs fully merge, probably long into the middle game.

More Data Needed for Deeper Comparisons

Perhaps decades from now there will be a sizable accumulation of chess960 games, some for each setup. It will be a long period of tantalizingly slow growth for each of the 960 setups. For the most recent year represented in my CD of chess games there are 64,000 games. Rounding 960 to 1,000 means each year would accumulate only 64 games per setup. But having chess960 gain formal recognition from the USCF and FIDE could mean at most half of the chess games would be chess960. Thus only 32 games per year would be captured for each setup. After several years there would be enough games to begin serious statistical comparisons between different setups.

The best comparisons would be between two setups that differ by only one attribute, if such an ideal is even possible. One example might be the two setups R#362-S#518 **RNBQ-KBNR** from chess1 versus R#330-S#230 **NRBQ-KBNR** (note columns a-b swapped). This comparison mostly isolates the effect of the 'a' wing knight being shifted one column further away from the center. But here there is also a change in knight opposition, which would not exist in R#330. Further, the ease for castling 'a' wing differs between the two. Comparisons involving R#362 would be inherently confounded anyway. One of the two setups would have been extensively analyzed for two centuries while the other has never yet been analyzed.

Another two comparable setups would be R#145 **QRNN-BKRB** versus R#305 **RQNN-BKRB**. Activation of the queens would be rather different between them. I think some people suspect White would have a higher ratio of wins to losses in R#145. The sharper the initial attacking options, the more White is thought to have a bigger advantage from his unfettered first move.

First Trend Faded to Fluke: For all of the Mainz 2005/08 chess960 games available in PGN, I tallied the number of pawn plies made separately by White and Black, just for games won by White. Then I repeated the task just for games won by Black. Then I repeated all those tallies for the Mainz 2005/08 chess1 games (same time control of Game/20 minutes +5 seconds delay). Admittedly this is less reliable than the analysis I described above, because 11 different setups were aggregated together to accumulate enough data for a comparison to chess1.

The results showed that in the games won by Black, each player averaged more pawn moves during the opening phase than when White won. White averaged 0.5 more pawn moves, and Black averaged 0.8 more. For comparison, the chess1 data showed that for games won by Black there were no pawn move count differences in comparison to chess1 games won by White. Before I could trust the finding for the chess960 data, I felt the need to find the same trend in another batch of games. So I repeated the tally process for the Mainz 2004/08 chess960 games. This time the chess960 data showed no differences between games won by White versus by Black. So the 2005/08 chess960 trend was not confirmed, and was probably due to the small amount of data available and to the variation effects of aggregating data from multiple chess960 setups.

Boundaries of our Imagination: Numerous statistical analyses become possible as a sufficient number chess960 game notations get captured in PGN files onto CDs, or are made downloadable from the web. It would be great to have enough that any fluke trends would have been overwhelmed by the relentless laws of probability. The only boundaries for possible statistical analyses may be our imagination.

In any database of chess games containing an opening tree, statistics are generated on which opening moves lead to the best (or worst) win-loss results. Of the four common first plies for White in chess1, win-loss statistics suggest 1. e24 may be the strongest. In chess960 it is almost certain that many setups are better played by something other than 1. e24. After enough chess960 game notations have been captured into databases we can start to find out which opening moves lead to the best results, in which types of initial setups. Such data may teach us something more about chess opening principles than we have learned from chess1 alone.

Suppose that from a large database of chess960 games, for each of the 960 setups, we measured the mean ply count at the point of the first queen movement. It is likely the data would plot to a bell curve. The few setups at the two extremes of the curve could be examined for features that may be the underlying cause of the ply count differences. Another type of analysis could compare this same measurement but just for the 120 setups that have the queen starting on say column 'f'.

We could generate an endless number of comparisons between setups. Each would have the potential to teach us something that truly deserves to be called chess opening theory.

Uncharted Waters

Next I will present some charts showing the results of statistical analyses I have run on data extracted from chess960 games. These charts are based on only a modest amount of data, so our conclusions from them must be regarded as tentative. I hope these charts convey a sense of the rich potential for statistical analyses between games from the various chess960 setups.

Castle Long, Redefinition: Chess960 finally gives us an opportunity to use appropriately the well-known chess phrase "castle long". In an exclusive chess1 world the phrases castling long and castling short are unnecessary and merely redundant to the phrases castling queen side and castling king side. In chess1 the king moves exactly two squares regardless of whether he castles 'a' wing or 'h' wing. But in chess960 there is a new concept for which the terms castling long and short are perfectly suited to help us. In chess960 a castling ply may move the king anywhere from 0 to 5 squares.

In chess960 castling long means the king castles to which ever column is further, 'c' or 'g'. If the White king starts on d1 and castles 'a' wing, thus moving to c1, then that king has castled short, because d1 is closer to c1 than to g1.

In chess1 history perhaps the phrase "castle long" came from the fact the 'a' column rook had to make a longer move during castling than did the 'h' rook. Or perhaps "castle long" came from the longer length of the old Descriptive notation O-O-O for 'a' wing castling, which is by two characters a longer notation than the old O-O for 'h' wing castling. Most algebraic notations used in chess1 adopt this same castling notation. Formal CRAN does not use the capital 'O'.

In chess960 castling notations, the notation O-O by itself can never inform us as to whether the castling was long or short. The notation O-O always means castling 'h' wing.

King Setup Position and 'h' Wing Castling: The following chart measures the number of 'h' wing castlings per game. Of course, the maximum is two per game. This measurement was taken for setups which varied in the number of pieces they require be moved out of the way before castling can occur, as tracked along the horizontal x-axis. For example in setup R#181-S#794 RQKN-BBRN (Mainz 2005/08 round 7), 2 pieces must move away before 'a' wing castling becomes possible (Qb1 Nd1). To enable 'h' wing castling 3 pieces must move away (Nd1 Be1 Bf1). So R#181 games are part of the x-axis group at value x=-1 (2-3=-1).

Chess960: Effect of the Pieces Blocking Castling.

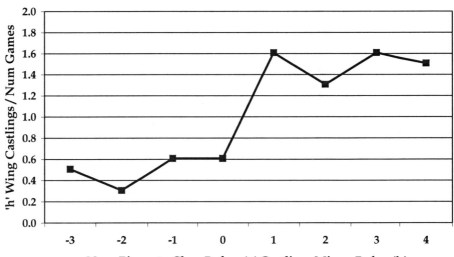

Num Pieces to Clear Before 'a' Castling, Minus Before 'h'.

One notable suggestion from the above chart is that there is one sharp change in the trend, from x-axis values 0 to 1. There does not seem to be a smooth transition from whether or not 'h' wing castling is popular, rather there is one big shift in popularity.

King Setup Position and Castling Long: When I first began to examine chess960 I expected to find some popularity for castling long, the most extreme case being Kb1g/R-f. For example a player could wait until his opponent accumulated attacking forces on the 'a' wing, then suddenly castle to the far away 'h' wing. The data may show some tendency to utilize this castle long option, but castling short is much more popular.

Popularities of Castling Long.

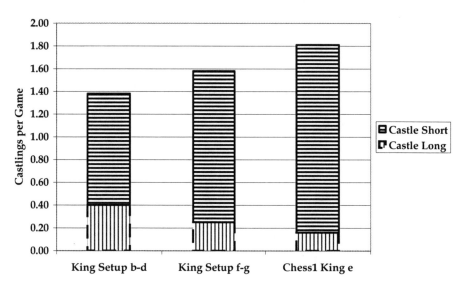

In the above chart there are three bar-pairs. The first two bar-pairs are from Mainz chess960 data, and the third is from Mainz chess1 data (so all time controls were Game/20 minutes +5 seconds delay). The three lower bars represent the rate of castling long (by our redefinition). In the chess1 case I treated 'a' wing as long. The three upper bars represent the rate of castling short. Both parts of each bar-pair combine to show the total rate of castling for their king setup square value along the x-axis. The maximum possible combined height is 2.0 (two castling plies per game).

The chart clearly shows castling short is much more popular than castling long.

The chart may show castling long is more popular in chess960 than is simple 'a' wing castling in chess1. The bottom segment of the right-most bar-pair shows that 'a' wing castling in chess1 is rare. That segment is smaller than the bottom segment in either of the two chess960 bar-pairs.

The above chart shows a persistent preference for 'h' wing castling over 'a' wing. We see from the bottom bars in the first two pairs, for a king that is setup adjacent to or on the castling destination 'c', the king is more likely to castle long (to the opposite wing) than when the king is setup near 'g'. Or, it might be counter-argued that all this data tendency shows is that the king setup on columns f-g is already on his exact castling short destination square more often than he is in the b-d case $(1/2 > 1/3)$. I am not persuaded by the counter-argument, because when the king is set up on b1 it is more difficult (by one added square) to castle long than when the king is setup on g1 (and there are several setups with Kb1 in the data). Players seem more willing to castle long to the 'h' wing than to castle long to the 'a' wing. This shows again the disdain of column 'c' as a castling destination for the king. As discussed earlier in this book, the chess960 castling rule should make the castling destination squares be g1 and b1 (not c1).

Let us compare the bottom segments from the two right-most bar-pairs. In chess960, with the king starting on the 'h' wing, 'a' wing castling occurs at a rate of 0.25 times per game. That is 56% higher than the 0.16 for chess1. What causes this unanticipated difference? One answer may be that the chess1 setup is wing symmetric, giving no motive for the king to castle to the wing that requires more squares first be cleared (3>2). However, it may be counter-argued that in chess960, with the king and rook starting on 'f' and 'c' respectively, that only the two squares d-e need to be cleared for 'a' wing castling (a-b can remain occupied). Thus 'a' wing castling is sometimes easier in chess960 compared to chess1. The weakness in the counter-argument is that with the king starting on 'f', 'h' side castling is extremely easy, yet 'a' wing castling grew in popularity.

A second answer may come from the psychological effects of playing chess960. I have not interviewed Levon Aronian, nor Peter Svidler, nor Bogdan Lalic (who helps by annotating his chess960 games in PGN). But given the opportunity I would ask them, "From any one typical chess960 setup, do you get a feeling that there are a wider variety of ways to conduct your pieces than in a chess1 game?" There is no less prize money at stake in Mainz in the annual FiNet Chess960 Open than in its sister chess1 event the Ordix Chess1 Open. The players want to win. They are not castling long to be funny or rambunctious. There may be a psychological effect from playing chess960 that emboldens one to more readily play non-ordinary strategies.

A third possible answer is that two centuries of analyzing the chess1 setup position has conditioned everyone to play only a small subset of the opening variations they would play if all that pre-game analysis had never occurred. Overall, we do not have a definitive answer in 2005.

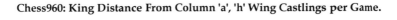

Chess960: King Distance From Column 'a', 'h' Wing Castlings per Game.

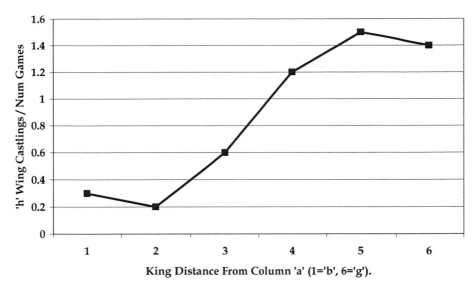

King Distance From Column 'a' (1='b', 6='g').

The chart immediately above is another angle to the same narrow idea. The primary feature to notice in this curve is how big a difference a single square can make. The steepest segment connects x-axis values 3 and 4 (king set up on 'd' or 'e'). When the king was set up on 'd' 3 squares away from column 'a', the games saw slightly more than a half player castle 'h' side (on average). The 'h' side castling rate doubled when the king was setup one additional square further from column 'a'.

Opposite Wing Castling: When both players castle but to different wings we call that "opposite wing castling". If the king is set up on column 'e' then this cannot be rephrased in terms of castling long or short. The chart below includes data only from games that featured opposite wing castling. The value range of the vertical y-axis could have been 0.0 thru 1.0 at its maximum, though for any one game the possible values are 0 or 1. The x-axis values derive from the king's start position relative to the 'a' column. If the king began on 'b' then that game was included in the 1 group; because 'b' is one square away from 'a'.

Proportion of Games Where White & Black Castled to Opposite Wings.

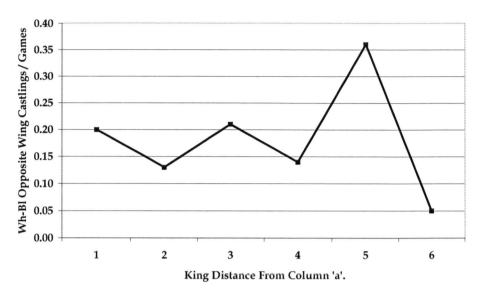

The above chart shows a steady rate of opposite wing castling for the 1-4 x-axis value range. That rate is about 17 times per 100 games. The data at x-axis value 4 fits both the chess960 data and data from Mainz chess1 as a control group. In fact my numbers were exactly the same for chess1: again chess960 is just chess.

The extreme data point at x-axis value 5 is based on very few games and so is unreliable. No surprise then that it is an outlier.

A Mega Database 2004 scan for chess1 games played at slow time controls showed a lower opposite wing castling rate of only 8%. All together, this chart plus the earlier charts hint that chess960 would lead to a slightly higher rate of opposite wing castling, compared to chess1.

The Simple Rate of Castling: The graph below suggests that players are more likely to castle if they can do so to the 'h' wing. It makes 'h' wing castling more difficult when the king starts on the 'a' wing (and the reverse). Plus we have seen a general preference for 'h' wing castling. Perhaps these two factors interact to create the modest trend present in the graph below.

Total Sum Castlings / Games

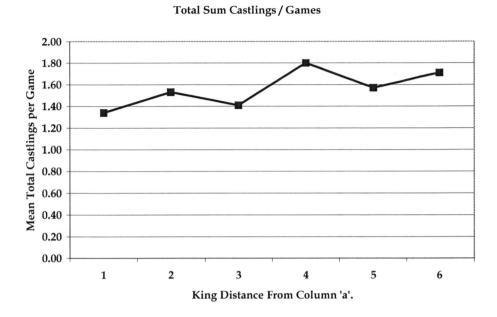

Mating Patterns Differ in the Middle Game
===

When chess960 rises in popularity there will also be an increased demand for chess960 books. As of 2005 mine is the third book published on chess960. People casually think there is no difference between chess960 and chess1 beyond the opening. Yet none of these three books have been devoted exclusively to the opening phase. My book deals with the opening phase extensively, but those chapters (7-8) are less than half of the book. Still more chess960 books about topics other than the opening phase will be needed.

King Fort Variation: One classification of chess960 books that will be needed concerns how to attack the castled king during the middle game. There are many chess1 books about how to attack the castled king. Those books focus on a few common king fort patterns that recur repetitiously in chess1. One such book I own is *How to Attack in Chess* by Gary Lane. Lane has a section devoted to attacking the traditional fianchettoed king fort, and another on the common tactical theme Bd3:h7# known as the "Greek gift". However, these chess1 books are specific to and limited to the few types of king forts that are natural for the chess1 setup. Most other chess960 setups have natural tendencies to form different kinds of king forts. In the future there will be an arms race in chess960, between king fort designers and those who study mating patterns against castled kings.

I tallied the degree of variation in king fort design between chess1 and chess960, sampling data from Mainz 2005/08. Even I was surprised by how narrow chess1 forts are compared to chess960 forts. For each rule set I calculated the **ratio of unique king forts divided by the number of castling moves, or Ukf/Ncm**. Here are the results (based on approximately 50 castling moves per rule set):

> 0.30 = Ukf/Ncm chess1
> 0.86 = Ukf/Ncm chess960

In chess960 it was a challenge to find any king fort design that was repeated in any other game. But in chess1, over 70% of the castling moves reused one of the three most common king fort designs.

The degree of fort variation in chess960 is even higher than the above numeric comparison suggests. In chess1 there were only a small number of 'a' wing castlings. But in chess960 there was a rich mix of 'a' wing plus 'h' castling. The fort designs on the 'a' wing tended to have more variation as a group, when compared to all the 'h' wing forts. By the way, the 'a' wing fort designs were usually not mere reverse images of 'h' wing forts.

In the next tiny diagrams, king forts taken from live Mainz play are displayed. All are shown as they were immediately after the castling ply was completed. All occurred from 'h' side castling. The chess1 diagrams show the four most common 'h' wing king fort designs in my tally. The chess960 diagrams show the kind of variation we are missing out on by not embracing both rule sets.

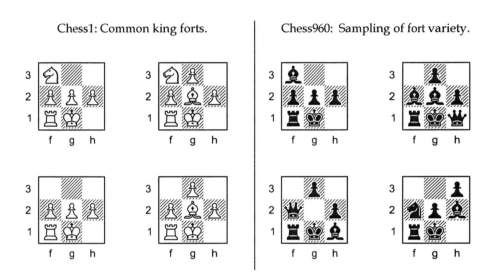

Chess1: Common king forts.　　Chess960: Sampling of fort variety.

These differences in chess960 forts, and presumably to their corresponding mating patterns, represent another important way in which the middle game phase is different between chess960 and chess1. Again, these differences are desirable. Chess960 can frequently bring us varieties we rarely get to see in chess1.

10
Influences on the Endgame

On their first exposure to chess960, most chess1 players find the chess960 setups and openings to be awkward or chaotic. Gligoric reports that in 1995, immediately after Anatoly Karpov played his first game of chess960, Karpov's tentative impression was that chess960 might lead to middle game positions that are not "harmonious". Now we inquire about the endgame. It is possible to reach strange or awkward endgame positions by legal moves. Does chess960 lead to awkward endgame positions? The answer is no.

As evidence, I expect that most readers will be able to determine which two of the following four diagrams came from live chess960 games. The other two diagrams were derived from composed chess problems (very slightly tweaked so there may be no precise solution). The composed diagrams demonstrate that it is possible for a legal endgame position to be awkward looking. The other two diagrams are simply from live chess960 play, and they look perfectly normal for chess1.

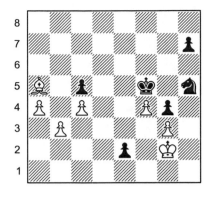

Diagram egk_50.

Diagram egk_51.

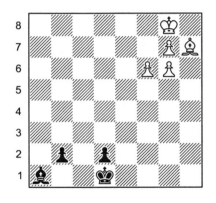

Diagram egk_52.

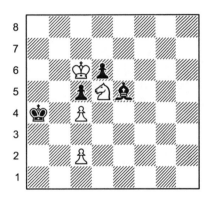

Diagram egk_53.

Let us look at this same idea from a different perspective. Shown next are two endgame diagrams from live play. One is from chess1 and the other from chess960 (R#448-S#145, BNRB-NQKR). I doubt there is any way to determine which diagram matches to which chess rule set.

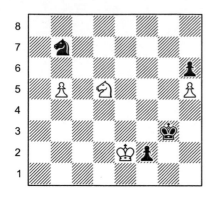

Diagram egy_60.

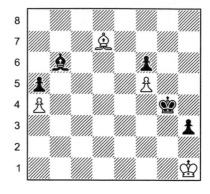

Diagram egy_61.

Any Endgame Differences?

Should we arrive at a quick conclusion that there are no endgame differences between chess1 and chess960? The above diagram comparisons would give some support to that conclusion. The few casual comments one can find searching the web certainly imply a consensus opinion that chess1 and chess960 have definitely and fully merged by the endgame, and probably much earlier. Yet I would like to argue that there might be endgame related differences. At the level of any one individual chess960 game I would agree that its endgame will be fully merged with chess1. Nonetheless in some ways chess960 remains distinct from chess1 even into the endgame.

When we examined the earlier phases of setup and opening and middle game, we performed useful comparisons between individual games from the two rule sets, and we found differences. When the endgame is reached, the fine granularity of individual game comparisons is no longer well suited to detecting the lingering differences. Instead it is time to consider the subject using aggregations of games.

Thought Experiment on Aggregations

Imagine an experimenter showed us two sets of endgame position diagrams. The sets are labeled AA and BB. Each set is devoted to one setup, either chess1 or R#136 BQNR-NKRB from chess960 (we avoid R#636 with its 'a' wing king). Only the experimenter knows set AA was from chess1, and BB was from R#136. Within those two setups, the games for display were chosen randomly, with the restriction that there be an approximate material equivalence between White and Black.

Would there be any way we could determine which diagram set came from chess1?

In theory, I suspect that we could determine which is the chess1 diagram set. We could find our own sample of say 1024 chess1 endgame positions. We could then catalog the frequencies of different endgame features. For example, how many endgames feature K+R+B v. K+R+N? Or in how many endgames are the kings located on opposite wings? Or how advanced is the average wing pawn and the average center column pawn? Then we could repeat that statistical work for 1024 endgames from R#136. If a couple of differences were then detectable between our two sets of frequency data, we could proceed to tally those same frequencies for sets AA and BB. If similar frequency differences appeared, we would be able to match AA and BB to our samples of size 1024, thus determining which unnamed sample was from chess1.

In practice there are not yet enough chess960 games in publicly available PGN files to support such a rigorous experiment. Even combining the two setups within one reciprocal-pair, and transposing the notations of half of them, would still not provide enough data. There are no chess960 games allowed in ChessGames.com. I did find 37 games of R#175-S#701 RQKB-NNBR on Chess-960.com but there were no R#675 games to transpose and treat as R#175. Many more games would be needed before reliable aggregations could be tallied.

Small Predictions: I will take a risk and make a few small predictions about the endgame differences that could be found between chess1 and chess960:

1. In chess1 R#362, the maneuver B-N5 (such as Bf8b4 or Bc1g5 etc) occurs with such a disproportionately high frequency that it likely leads to a disproportionate number of B:N occurrences. That N v. B imbalance should sometimes survive to the endgame. So I predict that a set of 1024 chess1 endgame diagrams would have relatively more N v. B endings than some other particular chess960 setups, and specifically R#136.

2. My second prediction is that R#136 would have fewer opposite shade B v. B endgames than would some other chess960 setups, maybe including chess1's R#362. The R#136 setup seems poised to exchange same shade bishops early in the game, with all the bishops staring at each other across the long diagonals.

3. I predict that R#136 would have more N v. N endgames than would chess1. This is because there is full knight opposition in chess1 but none in R#136. In theory, strong knight opposition should lead to more N:N exchanges and thus fewer knights come the endgame.

The understanding of aggregated endgame differences between chess1 and chess960 has its place in our academic understanding of chess. It might also modify our priorities in the types of endgames we study during the limited time we have available in our busy lives. But I doubt such information can be applied to advantage during tournament games. We should review what the great endgame master had to say about the final phase.

Foreseeing the Endgame

In his book *Last Lectures*, Jose Raoul Capablanca began his first chapter emphasizing and reemphasizing the connections between the opening and the endgame in chess1:

> "...*the opening must be studied in relation to the endgame.*" (Italics are Capablanca's.)

An underlying idea in that quotation has been expressed elsewhere using the phrase "organic whole". A well played chess game should be thought of as an organic whole, with the ideas linked and flowing logically in an uninterrupted manner between phases, from the opening through to the endgame.

> "...you cannot have a well-grounded understanding of the openings, nor can you satisfactorily appraise a great many of the current opening *variations* without an adequate knowledge of the endings." *(Italics mine.)*

Capablanca's point is that many chess1 opening variations have been found to offer mechanisms for creating one or more features that can favor one color come the endgame. Indeed some variations have been refined or designed to accomplish exactly this. Capa encourages players to learn about these endgame features, and then to study the opening variations that can create them. Further, once such a feature has been created during the opening, that feature should be protected and nurtured during the middle game so that it survives to the endgame. Together these techniques create a relationship between the non-contiguous phases of the opening and the endgame. Capa was writing about chess1, but should we presume these principles also apply to chess960?

Every chess1 player knows there is a strong relationship between the opening phase and the middle game. And everyone knows there is a strong relationship between the middle game phase and the endgame. These same direct relationships exist in chess960. Plus for chess960 we explicitly called out the previously implicit setup phase, which of course has a strong relationship to the opening phase. These relationships can be expressed by the "SOME" symbol set used below. These letters stand for Setup, Opening, Middle game, and Endgame.

chess1:	(S) → O → M → E
chess960:	S → O → M → E

The quotations from Capablanca are shifting our attention away from the simple direct relationships of O→M and M→E to the transitive relationship O→E:

$$O{\rightarrow}M \ \& \ M{\rightarrow}E, \ thus \ O{\rightarrow}E$$

O→E skips one node, M. When we look at this from the chess960 perspective we can see the two-node transitive relationship S→E:

$$S{\rightarrow}O \ \& \ O{\rightarrow}M \ \& \ M{\rightarrow}E, \ thus \ S{\rightarrow}E$$

Over the past half century the chess1 literature has supported the O→E relationship by documenting numerous opening variations designed to achieve endgame goals early in the game. We will be looking at those variations shortly below. Afterward we will try applying these chess1 O→E concepts to chess960.

Understanding O→E Exploitation
Then Abstracting for S→E

The subsections to follow describe how the O→E relationship can be exploited in chess1. We will see that most of the available techniques rely on opening variations that must be studied at home before the tournament. Since that approach is implausible in chess960, each subsection will be concluded with an attempt to identify a corresponding S→E abstraction that could be a useful substitute for memorized variations during live chess960 play.

To foretell our findings, these abstractions for chess960 do not seem to have as much practical value as do the concrete opening variations in chess1. This may call into question the presumption that the O→E relationship exists as strongly in chess960 as in chess1, at least as a practical matter.

[1] Clearing Away Queen Column Pawns for Early Q:Q: Edmar Mednis wrote a book entitled *From the Opening Into the Endgame*. One major option Mednis teaches to lower rated players is to seek a trade of queens in the opening against higher rated players. Mednis discusses specific variations of numerous chess1 openings including the English Opening (1. c24 without 1... c75) and the Pirc-ish Modern Defense. For instance, in the Modern Defense Mednis discussed the following variation:

1.	e24	g76	2.	d24	Bf8g7	3.	c24	d76
4.	Nb1c3	e75	5.	d4:e5	d6:e5	6.	Qd1:Q8#	
							(D10.1)	

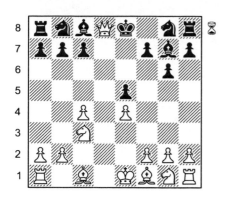

D10.1 Chess1, after 5... d6:e5 6. Qd1:Q8#.
Modern Defense.

White's 5. d4:e5 leads to a fully open 'd' column, allowing simplification by queen exchange.

With the queens gone, the endgame is much closer. Perhaps this opening strategy will give White a better chance to draw against a higher rated opponent.

This demonstrates the O→E link in chess1.

In his book *The Modern Defense* Vlastimil Hort gives two variations for very similar queen exchanges on page one.

For chess960 purposes we cannot give students variations to memorize. So we must try to formulate an abstraction of the underlying phenomenon that is common to many of the openings and variations Mednis describes. Phrased first for chess1 we might state the abstraction as:

> "The lower rated player should seek an opportunity to take with his 'd' pawn when the opponent must retake with his. Then the lower rated player should use the cleared 'd' column to exchange queens."

Indeed, above we saw 5. d4:e5 d6:e5 6. Qd1:Q8#. In variations from other openings the captures and recaptures can happen on square c5 instead of e5, as the exchange of queens is facilitated either way.

Rephrased more generally for chess960 we could state:

"The lower rated player should seek an opportunity to take with his queen pawn when the opponent must retake with his. Then the lower rated player should use the cleared queens' column to exchange queens."

We usually cannot force an exchange of queen pawns, though we can provide conditions that make it possible. The abstraction stated above could be of use during tournament games, especially to those who play postal chess960.

Early Queen Exchange in Chess960: Let us examine this abstract plan in chess960 action. One possible scenario might occur in R#532-S#091 NNRK-BRQB where White attempts to maximize the opportunities for the queen exchange along the 'g' column. I chose this setup because it happens to give White some tempo gaining initial moves to aid him in implementing his queen exchange plan. Other setups would likely be less supportive:

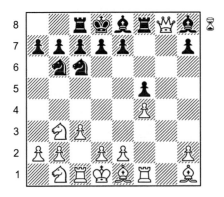
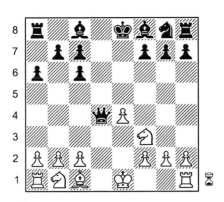

D10.2 R#532, after 6. Qg1:Q8.
Opening moves designed to jump
toward endgame by early
exchange of queens.

D10.3 Chess1, after 6... Qd8:Q4.
Ruy Lopez, exchange. var.
White jumps toward endgame
with 4. Bb5:Nc6 then 5. d24.

1. g24   Nb8c6   **2.** f24   Na8b6   **3.** c23   g76
4. Na1b3 f75   **5.** g4:f5 g6:f5   **6.** Qg1:Q8 **(D10.2)**

[2] Crippling a Wing Pawn Majority: In chess1 the Ruy Lopez opening has for centuries had a variation where White implements an endgame strategy on his fourth ply:

1. e24   e75   **2.** Ng1f3 Nb8c6   **3.** Bf1b5 a76
4. Bb5:Nc6 d7:Bc6   **5.** d24   e5:d4   **6.** Qd1:4 Qd8:Q4 **(D10.3)**
7. Nf3:Qd4

Here White has reduced the potential endgame power of Black's 'a' pawn majority, plus achieved an exchange of queens. White has good drawing chances against his higher rated opponent.

One key to creating this weakened island of Black 'a' wing pawns was tactical. In this situation Black needed to retake by moving his pawn diagonally toward the nearest wing edge. If Black's fourth ply could instead have been 4... b7:Bc6 (taking toward the central columns) then no crippled pawn island majority would have existed (just an isolated 'a' pawn).

This Ruy Lopez variation involves a fair amount of pre-conceived tactical coordination within the chess1 setup. I doubt there is any usable S→E abstraction for chess960 that we can take from this Ruy Lopez variation. These exact tactical moves are brittle in the sense that they cannot be applied to any other chess960 setup. The goal of crippling the opponent's wing pawn island majority applies to most if not all chess960 setups. Yet each setup requires its own tactical details for implementing such a long term strategy beginning in the opening phase, or even in the setup phase.

[3a] IQP - via the French Defense: In chess1 an IQP (isolated queen pawn) is often seen as an asset, although it takes skill to leverage this asset into a middle game advantage. An

IQP, like any other isolated pawn, can become a worsening weakness if an otherwise even endgame is reached. Eminent players disagree over whether the color having an IQP is at an overall advantage or disadvantage. Some very different types of chess1 openings can lead to an IQP.

The French Defense can lead to an IQP. Guided by his book *Pawn Power in Chess*, Hans Kmoch would say the variation below involves a "symmetrical" exchange of pawns at d5 (in plair 4), because both the taker and the re-taker were from the same neighboring 'e' column:

1.	e24	e76	2.	d24	d75	3.	Nb1d2	c75
4.	e4:d5	e6:d5	5.	Ng1f3	Nb8c6	6.	Bf1b5	Bf8d6
7.	d4:c5 (D10.4) Bd6:c5							

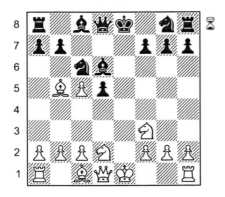

D10.4 Chess1, after 7. d4:c5.
French Def. White inflicts an
isolated queen pawn on Black,
potentially an endgame weakness.

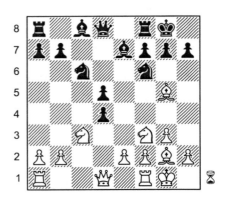

D10.5 Chess1, after 9... c5:d4
QGD Tarrasch var. Black accepts
an IQP. Use it to advantage during
the middle game, or risk endgame
disadvantage.

[3b] IQP - via the Tarrasch Variation of the Queen's Gambit Declined: An IQP similar to that seen in the French is generated by the Tarrasch variation of the Queen's Gambit

Declined, which uses a slightly different interaction of opposing rank 4 pawns. The crucial move is c75:

1. d24	d75	**2.** c24	e76	**3.** Nb1c3	c75
4. c4:d5 e6:d5		**5.** Ng1f3	Nb8c6	**6.** g23	Ng8f6
7. Bf1g2 Bf8e7		**8.** Ke1g/Rhf Ke8g/Rhf		**9.** Bc1g5 c5:d4 (D10.5)	

Is there any abstract technique or feature that is common to both of these IQP scenarios? The feature that seems common is the two abreast rank 4 pawns facing enemy pawns at their rank 3 and 4. This feature enabled the type of pawn exchanges White was seeking. Recall that further above we saw that two abreast rank 4 pawns were relevant to the Ruy Lopez variation for early queen exchanges (after 5. d24 Black's Pe5 was doubly attacked and was immobilized by White's Pe4). All this suggests the basic idea that when two advanced pawns stand shoulder to shoulder they enjoy a general flexibility that opens many options for their owner. Among these are options to influence the endgame. These options include the clearing of a column, the creation of a pawn island, and the creation of an isolated pawn.

[3c] IQP - via the Minority Attack: One of the better known opening strategies for inflicting an IQP on Black is through the minority attack, usually associated with the Queen's Gambit Declined in the 3. c4:d5 e6:d5 variation. Kmoch would call this an "unsymmetrical" pawn exchange:

1. d24	d75	**2.** c24	e76	**3.** c4:d5	e6:d5
4. Nb1c3	Ng8f6	**5.** Bc1g5	Bf8e7	**6.** e23	Ke8g/Rhf
7. Qd1c2	c76 (D10.6)	**8.** Bf1d3	Nb8d7	**9.** Ng1f3	Rf8e
10. Ke1g/Rhf h76		**11.** Bg5f4	Nd7f8	**12.** h23	Be7d6

200

13. Bf4:Bd6   Qd8:B6   **14.** Ra1b Bc8e6 **15.** b24   Qd6e7

16. b45   c6:b5 **(D10.7)**

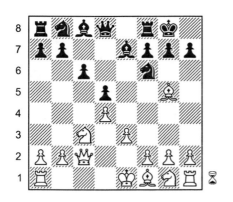

D10.6 Chess1, after 7... c76.
QGD, the opening moves have
set the stage for White to launch
a minority attack (b24 b45).

D10.7 Chess1, after 16... c6:b5.
QGD, the primary portion of the
minority attack is complete,
inflicting on Black an IQP on d5.

After 2. c24 and 3. c4:d5 we again see the two abreast rank 4 pawns discussed earlier exercising their options. In the present minority attack case, the direct infliction of a wing pawn weakness did not occur until plair 16, which is in the middle game. Yet the basis for the attack was intentionally constructed by plair 7, which is in the opening.

The conditions necessary for launching a minority attack are mostly pawn based. There is relatively little dependency on particular pieces being coordinated in one particular way. It is not necessary to memorize specific opening variations to initiate a minority attack. This makes the minority attack an exceptionally plausible carry-over opening strategy in chess960 from chess1.

Rethinking S→E for chess1

It would be a major challenge, even for strong chess players, to implement strategies in their live chess960 games based on the abstractions for S→E or just O→E discussed above. It is much easier to implement the O→E strategies in chess1 by leveraging the hard calculated variations available. Thus, in practical terms, the O→E relationship is stronger in chess1 than in chess960.

We should recognize that it is not the nature of R#362 that makes this true. Rather it is the long standing implicit pre-game announcement that R#362 will be used in chess1 that makes this true. In purely theoretical terms the O→E relationships are equally strong between the two chess rule sets. Further, in theory chess1 has an S→E relationship just as strongly as does chess960.

S→E Weaker in Chess960: In chess1 there can be an intimate relationship between the opening moves and the endgame imbalances that favor one color over the other. Chess960 has heightened our awareness of the links between the opening phase and the implicit setup phase. We see that some of those links are brittle and dependent on the particulars of the chess1 setup, while other links are flexible and applicable to many chess960 setups.

It is presumed that many or most chess960 setups each offer their own particular opening move variations that can exercise O→E links. These cannot plausibly be calculated during live chess960 play. Given that there are so many chess960 setups, it seems we should conclude that, in the practical sense, the O→E links will be weaker in chess960 than in chess1.

11
Winning Comparisons

The design of the chess1 rule set gives White an advantage toward winning. I see this as inherently unfair to the players, and undesirable for spectators. Those who created chess around 1475 could have prevented White's advantage with something like the FFM (Fair First Move) rule. In chess1 since 1965, White's advantage has led to more victories for White than for Black, by a ratio of 4/3= 1.33 (Watson, page 93). This means White accumulates 33% more wins than does Black. In this context 33% is a big number, and it violates the spirit of sporting competition. No wonder we hear frustrated players utter phrases like "I wasted a White". Or to paraphrase Watson: White feels an obligation to play for a win, but a draw with Black is considered an acceptable result. That many players feel this way when assigned the Black pieces is unhealthy for chess. We accept White's unfair advantage only because we were born into it.

The consensus from the chess960 grandmasters at Mainz is that the average chess960 setup gives White an even larger advantage than White has in chess1. Here are some quotations that articulate the consensus (from ChessTigers.de):

"I think that White has a huge advantage in the opening and the only way to reach an equal position with Black is to play symmetrical." (Peter Svidler, 2002)

"I think that White has a big advantage in the opening in some positions, Black should try to reach a symmetrical position." (Kiril Georgiev)

Neither player directly mentions what causes the increased advantage for White. Both suggest that Black would do better to mimic White's opening moves and play a symmetrical defense. I have rarely seen symmetrical play recommended for Black in chess1, beyond the Petroff Defense, and I suppose the Four Knights. I suspect they mean that, when White attacks early in the opening phase, Black should counter-attack rather than defend. Realistically those counter-attack opportunities exist only from symmetrical moves by Black. Ideally we would examine which chess960 setups are well suited to symmetrical openings by Black, but that is further than I am willing to go in this book.

At the moment I want to examine the central claim in the above quotations. Is it really true that White has an increased advantage in chess960 compared to chess1? We have enough data to begin to test this consensus opinion.

In the table below there are two types of calculations presented. "Wh/Bl" is the number of 1-0 outcomes divided by the number of 0-1 outcomes (White wins divided by Black wins). "Draw" is the number of draws divided by the total number of games.

	Chess1		Chess960
	1880's	**Present Day**	**Present Day**
Game/ 20 min	(null)	Wh/Bl = **1.27** Draw = **0.23**	Wh/Bl = **1.13** Draw = **0.19**
Slow Time	Wh/Bl = **1.17** Draw = **0.28**	Wh/Bl = **1.33** Draw = **0.30**	(null)

Effect of Errors: An initial observation is that the Wh/Bl ratio is smaller for rapid chess1 than for regular slow chess1. I interpret this comparison as revealing there are more errors made during rapid play than during slow play, hardly a surprise. Errors are like uncontrolled variability in a science experiment, in that they tend to dilute any effect being measured. Here they dilute the effect of White's first move advantage.

We would expect more errors in rapid chess960 than in rapid chess1. If that leads to further dilution, we should see a still lower Wh/Bl ratio, and indeed we do. Thus we have an answer: no (1.13 < 1.27). White does not have an increased advantage in chess960, at least in practice. Yet in theory, if humans were able to deeply study all 960 setups and remember all their prepared variations, we might see a higher Wh/Bl ratio in chess960 than in chess1. Where chess960 is concerned, the practical trumps the theoretical.

Early Tactics: Tactical challenges can arise very quickly in any chess game. Tactics arise from the third ply in several chess1 openings. In the Ruy Lopez, 1. e24 e75 2. Ng1f3 initiates a tactical concern that can lead to a long sequence of tactical issues. In the King's Gambit, 1. e24 e75 2. f24, Black must already calculate against unleashing a large development advantage for White. In Alekhine's Defense, 1. e24 Ng8f6, plair 1 has already raised tactical questions.

Yet all these chess1 examples involve short range pieces (pawn and knight). The chess1 setup does not provide White much potential for quick tactical threats using long range pieces. The best it offers may be 1. e24 e75 2. Bf1c4 Bf8c5 3. Qd1h5, which leaves White with positional problems.

In contrast many of the chess960 setups do provide for quick threats from long range pieces, namely from the bishops and queen. Also, these threats can arise even earlier, after the first ply instead of the fifth or the third. Any setup containing a bishop or queen on columns a,b,g,h might offer a tactical threat from the very first ply. One example is R#513-S#447 RNNB-KRBQ, after 1. g23, threatening Qh1:b7.

In chess960, perhaps White is perceived to have an even bigger advantage than in chess1 for two reasons. First, White can initiate tactical threats earlier, even on the first ply. Second, those tactical threats emanate from long range pieces. White is perceived to have a bigger advantage in chess960 because White can initiate tactical threats with long range pieces on ply 1.

A Granular Examination of Win-Lose-Draw Rates per Setup

Perhaps the comments by Svidler and Georgiev were motivated in part by one or two setups they used that seemed to favor White exceptionally. With data tallied from Mainz, the table shows the setups which gave White the biggest advantage, as judged by win-loss data (especially R#018). Also shown are the setups in which Black did the best (especially R#795). In the second half of the table the setups with the highest and lowest draw rates are listed (R#932 and R#130).

Table: Mainz Chess960 Setups Yielding Exceptional Trends

yyyy/mm Round	Setup Id	Setup String	Wh/Bl -or- (Bl/Wh)	Draw Rate: High -or- (Low)
			*D11.1	
2002/08 rd.2	R#018- S#768	BBQR- KNRN	4.33	0.24
2003/08 rd.9	R#835- S#632	RBNK- BQRN	2.57	0.26
2002/08 rd.4	R#161- S#699	RQKN- BNRB	2.00	0.25
2005/08 rd.11	R#708- S#651	RNKR- BQNB	1.89	0.16
			*D11.2	
2002/08 rd.8	R#795- S#832	BBRK- NRQN	(2.00)	0.10
2005/08 rd.2	R#448- S#145	BNRB- NQKR	(1.56)	0.12
2003/08 rd.3	R#155- S#393	QRNB- BNKR	(1.45)	0.21
2004/08 rd.11	R#564- S#379	NRKR- BNQB	(1.33)	0.24
				*D11.3
2004/08 rd.4	R#932- S#907	RKQR- BNNB	1.00	0.35
2002/08 rd.9	R#529- S#189	NRNB- KRBQ	1.29	0.27
2003/08 rd.11	R#309- S#410	RQNN- BBKR	0.92	0.26 *D11.11 – 13
				*D11.4

2005/08 rd9	R#130- S#096	BBQN- RNKR	1.38	(0.06)
2004/08 rd.2	R#890- S#346	NRKQ- BBRN	1.07	(0.12)
2003/08 rd.5	R#628- S#859	RKNR- BNQB	0.85	(0.12)
2004/08 rd.6	R#112- S#001	BQNB- NRKR	1.00	(0.13)

The sample sizes for the chess960 setups are smaller than we would like. For any one setup there is a risk that what data we have is a misleading fluke. I compared the variability among chess960 rounds against the variability among chess1 rounds. I found there was more variability among the chess960 rounds: the Wh/Bl ranges were similar, but the chess1 data had a lower frequency of outliers. I interpret this to mean that the different setups in the chess960 were having varying effects on White's advantage.

Next, all of these setups are displayed in diagrams for easier visual comparison. Perhaps it would have made the comparisons easier if I had shown each setup as the member of its reciprocal-pair that has the king on the 'h' half of the row (columns e-g). I rejected the idea in case the minor castling rule asymmetry between 'a' and 'h' wing matters.

In each crowded diagram, the first setup Id listed in the caption is in the top row, row 7. Each top row is the most extreme for its category.

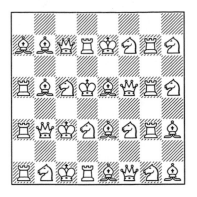

D11.1 White advantage Wh/Bl.
R#018, R#835, R#161, R#708.

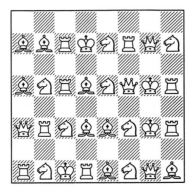

D11.2 Black advantage (Wh/Bl).
R#795, R#448, R#155, R#564.

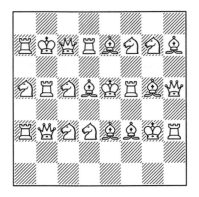

D11.3 Highest draw rates.
R#944, R#529, R#309 (in row 3).

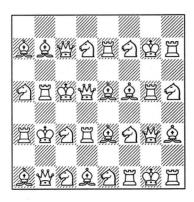

D11.4 Lowest draw rates.
R#130, R#890, R#628, R#112.

Answering Why

Attribute Tables: Is it reasonable to hope we could stare at the group of Wh/Bl setups and somehow see or sense why White won twice as many games as Black? When I first casually tried this I briefly thought most of these setups have a corner bishop and that might be the crucial factor. After another minute of looking the corner bishop theory collapsed. A glance at the setups where Black won more games also shows corner bishops. Every 7 of 16 chess960 games will have a corner bishop, so there is nothing special about such setups.

Is knight opposition the crucial factor? No. Half of the Wh/Bl setups have knight opposition and half do not. I filled out setup attribute tables, as part of an attempt to assess each attribute's contribution to White's advantage. Unfortunately I noticed no correlations or patterns.

Diagrams of Decisive Positions for Wh/Bl: What we have left is the individual game notations from these exceptional rounds. In the diagram set below, each diagram is from a different setup that indicated a strong advantage for White. Each shows the crucial position near the moment when White obtained his clear advantage. Perhaps we could glean the reasons White dominated in these setups if we examine these crucial positions in the context of their whole game. This will be attempted for the first two diagrammed games.

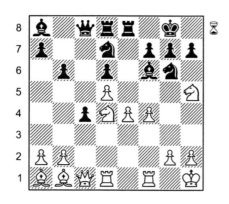

D11.5 S.Galdunts – P.Svidler, 1-0
Mainz 2002, R#018, Wh/Bl.
After 13. Ne2d4 +.8
Next 13... Qc85? +1.6 14. Nd4f5

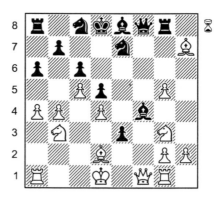

D11.6 K.Landa – B.Lalic, 1-0
Mainz 2003, R#835, Wh/Bl.
After 14. Bc2:h7 +.5
Next 14... Rg8h? +1.3 (Bf4:Ng3 -.2)

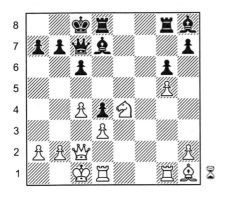

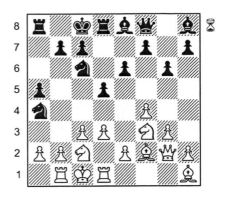

D11.7 R.Vaganian – P.Tregubov, 1-0
Mainz 2002, R#161, Wh/Bl.
After 17. Kc1/Rad Be8d7? +.6 (Rg8f -.6)
Next 18. Ne4c5 Bh8e5

D11.8 K.Bischoff – I.Sokolov, 1-0
Mainz 2005, R#708, Wh/Bl.
After 9... a75 10. Qf1g2 +.2
Next 10... Bh8:c3!? +.5 11. b2:Bc3 Na4:c3

Chess Game Annotation Format: Below is a table of the complete Galdunts-Svidler R#018 game. This table shows annotations for each ply, courtesy of the Chispa 4.03 chess engine (coded by Federico Corigliano), installed and managed by the Arena windowed program (coded by Martin Blume, PlayWithArena.com). Both programs are free. The disregard long shown for chess960 by the major commercial chess programs created an opportunity for several free programs to gain exposure by becoming indispensable alternatives. These programs include Arena and Chispa and Spike.

The moves Chispa would have made are in the shaded columns on the right portion of the table. These can be compared to the actual moves made by the players. An annotation of '=' means the chess engine recommended the same move actually made by the player.

A '+' by itself indicates White is better by some undetermined amount, though probably not a large or decisive amount. A '-' indicates Black is better. A '++' means White is much better and has a decisive advantage. A "+.4" means the move leaves (or would have left) White ahead by almost a half pawn. All evaluation values are shown to the level of a tenth of a pawn, there being no genuine difference between +.21 and +.24. Chess engines never give out '!' annotations, only '?'.

In the game below, the "Chispa White" entries for plairs 13-14 reveal that Black's 13th ply may have been the losing move. It was there that the evaluation jumped from +.8 to +1.6.

S.Galdunts – P.Svidler, 1-0
R#018-S#768 BBQR-KNRN
Mainz 2002/08, Rd.2, Wh/Bl=4.33.

	Actual White	Actual Black	Chispa White	Chispa Black
1.	c24	b76		
2.	Nh1g3	Nh8g6		
3.	d24	e76		=
4.	e24	c75 (Qc8:5 good for Black.)	Nf1d2	=
5.	d45	Bb8e5 (Cannot dislodge in 1 ply, protects Pg7, hampers b23.)	d4:c5	Ng6f4 (Attack Pg2.)
6.	Ng3e2	d76	Nf1d2	Qc87 +.1
7.	f24	Be5f6	Nf1g3 +.4	=, +.2
8.	Nf1g3	e6:d5	d5:e6 +.3	e65 +.3
9.	c4:d5? (Ba8-b7-a6 possible.)	Nf8d7 (Black cramped by Pd5. Knights both wanted g6.)	e4:d5 +.6	=, +.3
10.	Ke1g/Rgf	Ke8g/Rgf	=, +.3	Ba8b7 +.4

11. Ng3h5	Rf8e	=, +.3	Bf6e7 +.3
12. Kg1h	c54?	Nh5:Bf6# +.4	Bf6e7 +.2
13. Ne2d4 (D11.5)	Qc85?	Ne2g3 +.8	Bf6:Nd4 +.7
14. Nd4f5	Ng6e7?	=, +1.6	Qc57 +1.7
15. Nf5:g7 (D11.9)	1-0	=, +4.5	Bf6:Ng7 +4.3
16.		Nh5:Bg7	f76
17.		Ng7e6++	

Stronger for Black might have been 12... Bf6e7 13. b23 Be7f8 14. Qc1b2 f76 15. f45 Ng6e5 +.2.

Why did Svidler as Black lose the above game? White's advanced center pawns gave White a space advantage. That created an unforgiving situation by the time Black made the questionable moves in the crucial position.

The setup R#018 has an adjacent bishop pair in the corner, offering a hypermodern approach to the center. Chess960 setups having this attribute seem to reward players who use their adjacent corner bishops to support their advanced center pawns d-e. This level of double bishop support for one's center pawns is harder to achieve in the chess1 setup. Galdunts had sort of a hyper-classic center. Galdunts had all the support he needed for advancing his center pawns from the discovered pressure of his own rank 1 pieces. The centered pawns will block corner bishops of both colors. So a player should try for a central space advantage if he can, and not worry excessively about his own blocked bishop. The middle game can provide ways to mobilize those center pawns when the time is right.

Did the setup R#018 give White an advantage that enabled Galdunts to cramp Black? I would say no. White had three rank 4 pawns before Black had any, but this was by Black's choice. White had no threats of any kind restricting Black's options until perhaps plair 11. Maybe 1... c75 would have been a better move for Black. When it came later White was already in position to scoot by the challenge with d45.

Black's 13... Qc85? pressured White's Nd4 away, but to an even deeper penetrating outpost on f5. Black's pieces were cramped by White's center pawns, and Black was unable to pressure square f5. In chess1 Black is used to having Bc8 in the initial setup, available to press f5. But in R#018 it is harmful to have an automatic feeling that an enemy move N-f5 can be repulsed. Similarly our chess1 experiences give us little or no practice at attack patterns against the Black king involving White N-h5 (as in White's ply 11). In chess960 this maneuver continues to recur when the setup starts with Nh1. Watson (page 157) noted "Modern players have no inhibitions about placing knights on the edge...". In chess960 it can be natural to place knights on the edge.

We should keep in mind that the time control was Game/20 with a +5 second delay. At rapid speeds there will be erroneous moves made even by great players. Plus I think the players enjoy the chess960 games and like experimenting with them. They are more willing to take risks in hopes of learning something from the outcome.

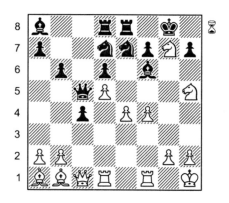

D11.9 S.Galdunts – P.Svidler, R#018
FINAL 1-0, after 15. Nf5:g7

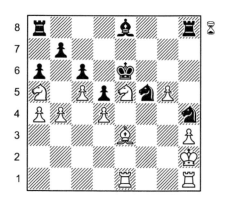

D11.10 K.Landa – B.Lalic, R#835
FINAL 1-0, after 27. Rf1h?

According to our statistics, the next game we look at also uses a setup that may increase White's advantage of unfettered first move. Immediately above here are the final position diagrams for the game above and the game below.

K.Landa – B.Lalic, 1-0
R#835-S#632 RBNK-BQRN
Mainz 2003/08, Rd.9, Wh/Bl=2.57.

	Actual White	Actual Black	Chispa White	Chispa Black
1.	c24	Nh8g6		
2.	Nh1g3	c76		
3.	d24	d75		
4.	c45	e75		
5.	e23	e54		
6.	f24	f75		
7.	b24	Ng6e7 (Nc8 may want e7.)		
8.	Nc1b3	Bb8c7		
9.	a24	a76		
10.	Bb1c2	g75 (Black cannot castle.)	Qf12 +.1	Qf86 +.1
11.	f4:g5	f54	Ng3e2 +.1	Rg8:5 -.1
12.	e3:f4	Bc7:f4	=, +.2	Qf8:4 +.3
13.	Be1d2	e43?	=, +.1	Bf4:Bd2 +.2
14.	**Bc2:h7?** (D11.6)	Rg8h?	Bd2c1 +.9	Bf4:Ng3 -.2
15.	Ng3e2	Rh8:B7?	=, +.7	Bf4:g5 +.7
16.	Ne2:Bf4	Qf85	Bd2:e3 +2.3	=, +2.0

17. Bd2:e3	Rh7:2	=, +2.0	=, +2.0
18. Qf13	Ne7g6	Kd12 +2.2	Kd87 +2.2
19. Kd1g/Rgf	Rh27	=, +2.3	=, +2.3
20. Nb3a5	Ng6h4	Nf4:Ng6 +2.2	Ng6:Nf4 +2.2
21. Qf3h	Qf5:Qh3	Qf3g +2.6	=, +2.6
22. g2:Qh3	Kd87	=, +2.5	=, +2.5
23. Kg1h2	Nc8e7	Na5:b7 +2.8	=, +2.3
24. Nf4d3	Ne7f5	=, 2.3	Nh4f5 +2.4
25. Nd3e5#	Kd7e6?	Ra1e +2.5	Kd7c +2.6
26. Ra1e	Rh78	=, +5.5	Ke67 +6.5
27. Rf1h? (D11.10)	1-0	Be3f2 +7.6	Ke67 +3.6

A stronger finish could have been 27. Be3f2 clearing column 'e' for threats of discovered check. No good for Black is 27... Nh4f3# (essentially trapped) 28. Ne5:Nf3# Ke6d7 29. Nf3e5# leaving Black down a knight. Also no good for Black is 27... Be8h5 28. Bf2:Nh4 Nf5:Bh4 29. Ne5:c6# announcing mate in 7 plairs.

Why did Lalic as Black lose the above game? After 5. e23 Landa as White had dim prospects for a king fort. There was too much vertical separation between the White king and its protective 'a' wing pawns. As positional compensation White got a space advantage on the 'a' wing. More importantly White had great open lines for his pieces, and Black did not.

Black advanced and sacrificed his 'h' wing pawns to open lines for his pieces. With 12. Bc7f4 it looked like Black might begin a successful attack on White's exposed king. Instead, White was able to exchange off Black's active pieces, leaving only Black's pawn material deficit.

I have not quantified it, but informally I feel some chess960 setups show a high rate of wing pawn advances of the sort launched above by Landa as White. John Watson noted a couple of times that early advances of the pawns protecting the castled king have slowly become more acceptable in the decades since Nimzovich wrote *My System*. From page 137, "...strictures against flank advances in undeveloped positions are quite as limiting of the chess imagination as are other rules...". Had chess960 been installed in 1475 perhaps it would not have taken the combined chess community a century to realize this. I wonder whether the future might bring a book entitled *The Latest Secrets of Chess Strategy: Advances Since Watson*, or whether all strategic ideas of chess have already been discovered and properly weighted. If there is more to learn, I believe chess960 could help accelerate the rate of discovery.

Overall the outcome of this game was determined by the interaction of Black's aggressive and almost experimental pawn play on the 'h' wing. Part of this pawn play was 7... Ng6e7 and 10... g75. Together these moves neglected the fundamental law of chess that you must protect your king. Black's neglect of king safety was not caused by the setup R#835.

Summary of Wh/Bl Conclusions: I do not feel there is enough data for me to draw any conclusions about why R#018 or R#835 showed such a lopsided advantage for White. The games we analyzed were lost due to questionable choices made by the Black players, not due to any setup attributes. Until masters play more games of chess960 we may have to settle for the enjoyment of searching for explanations.

Examining Draw Prone Setups

It is time to perform the same investigational technique on the most draw prone setups. This is just barely possible because relatively few drawn games were published by Chess Tigers, echoing standard practice in the chess world. Also, before 2005 their chess960 PGN files available for download contained some format errors that were not resolvable.

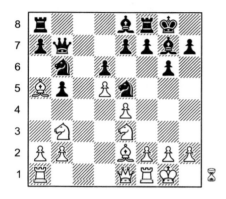

D11.11 A.Yusupov – V.Iordachescu, .5-.5
Mainz 2003, R#309, High Draw rate.
After 12. Kf1g/Rhf Nc8b6 +.7
Next 13. Ba5c3 Ra8c.

D11.12 A.Dreev – V.Zvjaginsev, .5-.5
Mainz 2003, R#309, High Draw rate
After 18. Be1f2 Rd87 +.8
Next 19. Ra1d Qb8d6.

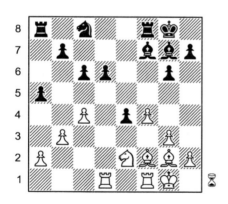

D11.13 K.Landa – Z.Varga, .5-.5
Mainz 2003, R#309, High Draw rate.
After 17. Nc3:Ne4 f5:Ne4 +.2
Next 18. Bg2:e4 a54.

R#309. Three drawn games (**D11.11 – 13**), perhaps due partly to their high quality king forts. This interesting double bishop style king fort is extremely rare in chess1, but is common in some other setups. The other forts are common in chess1.

218

The only drawn game published for the most draw prone setup, R#944, has an invalid PGN file. The only draw available for the next most draw prone setup, R#529, suffered from impossible PGN moves which I could not reconstruct. Castling was a problem for PGN capture until Mainz 2005/08. Perhaps I could have manually fixed these files if the PGN specification called for CRAN instead of a less informative notation.

These positions above from setup R#309 continued into hard fought games. Perhaps R#309 was draw prone because it allowed for strong king forts. The double bishop style seen above in four of the six positions is highly unusual in chess1, but clearly there are other setups which tend to facilitate or encourage this refreshing novel formation.

This king fort trend makes me look again at the Wh/Bl positions further above. Of those four Wh/Bl position diagrams only the Vaganian–Tregubov R#161 game featured fine king forts. So perhaps a pair of low quality king forts gives White's advantage of first move a greater chance of translating into victory.

Oddly Located Rank 2 Weaknesses

From repeated exposure to the chess1 setup we all know that the two KB2 squares, f2 and f7, are inherent weak points on each color's rank 2. We have less intuitive understanding of where the weak points are in chess960 setups. Consider the following Bacrot-Ruck game also from Mainz 2005/08 R#708. Notice how weak points at c7 and e7 emerge, and are swiftly and cleverly exploited by White.

E.Bacrot – R.Ruck, 1-0
R#708-S#651 RNKR-BQNB
Mainz 2005/08, Rd.11, Wh/Bl=1.89.

	Actual White	Actual Black	Chispa White	Chispa Black
1.	Nb1c3	d75		
2.	d24	Ng8f6		
3.	g24	e76		Nf6:g4 +.1
4.	g45	Nf6d7	=, +.1	=, +.2
5.	Qf1h3	Qf8g?	e24 +.1	h76 +.1
6.	e24?	c76?	Bh1:d5 +1.1	d5:e4 +.3
7.	e4:d5	c6:d5 (D11.14)	=, +1.3	=, +1.3
8.	Bh1:d5!	e6:Bd5?	=, +1.3	Nb8c6 +1.3
9.	Nc3:d5	Nb8c6	Threatens Nd5e7 fork.	=, +2.0
10.	Qh3g	Nd7e5	Coordinates on c7.	=, +2.0
11.	d4:Ne5	Rd87	=, +2.0	=, +2.0
12.	c24	Kc1/Rad	White went on to win with a pawn material advantage.	

Why did Ruck as Black get into trouble? One answer is that Black had to play against the ninth highest rated chess player on the planet. More directly, Black's 5... Qf8g put his K and Q on squares of the same shade, and it weakened square e7. These factors primed the knight fork threat at the weakened e7 square. The inherent weakness in R#708 at c7 was also exploited by the coordination of 9. Nc3:d5 and 10. Qh3g. In chess1 both pieces setup adjacent to the king protect the square in front of the king, but not so in R#708 RNKR-BQNB.

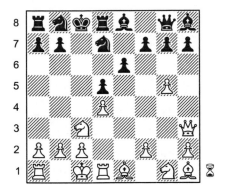

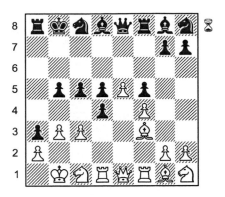

D11.14 E.Bacrot – R.Ruck, 1-0
Mainz 2005, R#708, Wh/Bl
After 7. e4:d5 c6:d5 +1.3
Next 8. Bh1:d5! e6:Bd5? +2.0

D11.15 A.Kosteniuk – I.Sokolov, 0-1
Mainz 2005, R#913-S#829, Pawn Plies
After 10... b65 11. c23. Next 11... Nh8g6
+.6 12. Nc1d3? -.2 (c3:d4 +.6) c54

After the first eight plairs were completed, Black still had seven of his eight pieces on his rank 1, and none enjoyed a single open line of mobility or pressure. Black's king sat on a pawn-less diagonal, and was several moves away from castling. White's sacrificial combination launched by 8. Bh1:d5! made possible the devastating penetration of White's knight.

Numerous Early Pawn Moves: As long as we are tangentially touching on the topic of chess960 games that open with numerous pawn moves, we can for fun also glance at the R#913 RKNB-QRBN game between Kosteniuk – Sokolov (**D11.15**). After the first 21 plies the opening phase was nearly over, and Sokolov had yet to move any non-pawn piece (any "officer"). Alexandra was violating the classic Nimzovich opening principle against excessive pawn moves to almost the same degree, as she had only one vacant rank 1 square. All four knights were on their initial square. This odd game also showed how readily chess960 players sometimes abandon their hopes of a high quality king fort.

Conclusions About White's Advantage

The Chess Tigers in Mainz cannot capture in PGN the moves of all the chess960 games between titled players, because DGT equipment is expensive. The Chess Tigers do publish the simple win-lose-draw outcome of every game. So we have now an accumulation of game outcomes, enough to test the consensus that White's average advantage in chess960 is even larger than White's advantage in chess1. I believe the data refute that consensus. Note that it would not be a contradiction for there to be a subset of chess960 setups which do increase White's advantage. My gut feeling is there are some chess960 setups that probably do enhance White's unfair advantage more than some other setups.

On the simplest of statistical ideas it is likely that the chess1 setup is somewhere in the middle between the two extremes. So some chess960 setups probably give White a smaller advantage than does the chess1 setup. The Mainz chess960 data guided us to examine a few setups which may enhance White's advantage. But our attempts to glean why those particular setups enhance White's advantage were unable to latch onto anything specific. Setup characteristics that looked promising were undercut by plentiful counter examples. Actual games are each driven by their own particulars. White's excessive victory count seemed to come only from questionable choices made by Black. If there is any abstract commonality between those games, derived from the setup, it is probably stretched so thin as to be useless as an explanation. Still, any reliable pattern happens for a reason. I have a feeling that king fort quality may be an operative factor, but I cannot yet go so far as to make that assertion. The issue could be reexamined after more master chess games are captured into PGN files in the coming years.

12
Reviewing Our Broadened Understanding of Chess

Chess960 is an Incremental Change: In this book chess960 has been used to gain a better perspective and understanding of chess1, and of chess. Chess was not revised in the year 1475, rather chess was invented in 1475. Like most human inventions, chess was merely an incremental step above several similar games that preceded it. The changes that created chess were radical in that half the pieces were discarded and replaced by more mobile pieces (though the same names were reused).

In 1996 Bobby Fischer invented FRC. Like most human inventions, FRC was merely an incremental step above several similar ideas that preceded it. This change was miniscule compared to the changes of 1475. FRC is exactly one rule change, that in the initial setup the rank 1 pieces need not be lined up the same way every time.

The FRC proposal could be viewed as chess borrowing the 3-Move rule change adopted for checkers in the early 1900's.

The extreme success of the checkers 3-Move rule may call into question the quick rejections some people have expressed against FRC.

Whereas Fischer's motivations for FRC could be described as negative (fixing broken chess1), one central thesis in this book is that there are also many positive reasons to nurture FRC, and that the positive reasons are even more compelling than the negative reasons.

Chess Tigers Demonstrate the Positives of Chess960: The Chess Tigers in Mainz, Germany have done so much excellent work at promoting FRC, now chess960, that they should be considered the co-founders of chess960.

By studying the games of the many masters and grandmasters that attend the annual Mainz chess960, we can see that the middle game is different than in chess1. Yet the players consistently report that the chess960 middle games feel fully proper for chess. This apparent paradox is understood by realizing that chess1 is the odd implementation of chess, and that chess960 is more natural. Chess1 is a severe subset of chess. Not only does chess1 limit us to one initial setup, that one setup is symmetrical. There is no reason why chess960 middle games even could feel improper for chess. The same pieces are used with all the same rules. Chess960 allows the pieces to express the full richness of chess.

While all would expect the moves of the opening phase to be different in chess960, many players might be surprised that the principles of opening phase play are also different in chess960.

There is much that needs to be researched and published about chess960. These future publications will broaden and deepen our understanding of chess in general. The chess1 literature alone could never provide all the perspectives and insights about chess that chess960 publications will.

Fischer said "old chess is dead", but I disagree. I agree with Fischer that chess1 does have problems caused by its static initial setup, and that those problems are growing. Yet chess1 continues to show humanity the extremes of excellent play that are possible in chess. By freezing the initial setup for all chess1 games, masters have been able to treat chess1 partly like a puzzle to be solved at home. This has greatly advanced our understanding of what perfect opening phase play can be like. However, for a digital sport like chess, this puzzle aspect damages the dignity of chess1 as a sport. Chess960 accepts imperfect opening play in exchange for a more sporting form of chess, one that offers advantages to chess spectators. Indeed, I made a reasoned argument that, in an important albeit narrow way, Chess is the greatest spectator sport of all time.

Chess960 Rules: I gave a formal statement of the rules of chess960. This included descriptions of the R# and S# setup Id systems. I went further and discussed proposals for improving chess960. The Fair First Move (FFM) rule suggestion shows that White's unfair advantage exists only if we let it.

The draw problem in chess is really multiple problems. The Draw Offer Duration 2 (DOD2) rule suggestion is a painless way to reduce the draw problems in chess generally.

The most damaging problem is that two evenly matched grandmasters often have their games end in a draw, despite the aggressive efforts of each to win. The suggested Opposite Wing Castling (OWC) rule, combined with chess960, gives us an extremely rare opportunity to increase the asymmetries of chess in a natural manner that is fair to both players.

The old specifications for chess game notation files are not robust enough to accommodate chess960 without modification. I described the trade-off choices being debated for the FEN portion of PGN files.

Chess960 Itself Examined: A belief often stated is that chess960 will eliminate the need to study the opening phase. I strongly doubt this. It even implies that grandmasters could never improve the quality of their chess960 opening play, which again I strongly doubt. Necessity is the mother of invention, and new approaches to studying the opening phase will be needed. This book described the approach of Setup Attributes assessment, as a way of guiding the earliest moves toward narrow short-term goals.

Some have called for the elimination of certain classes of setups. Yet if we were to union together all the calls to eliminate some setups, there might be only one setup left. Setups with bishops in the corners have been criticized by some. Yet setups with corner bishops, including R#731, can be laden with interesting challenges and dilemmas for each player. Chess1 rarely lets us experience these challenges, either as players or as spectators. The contrasts between play from different setups, like between R#731 and R#155, provide instructive   feedback   that   accelerates   our   deepening comprehension of general chess principles.

I examined the various phases of a typical chess game. I explicitly called out the setup phase that has always preceded the opening phase. I argued that the 960 setups cannot usefully be categorized. Instead, I offered a system of attribute analysis for setups. Examples of cataloging the attribute analysis of a setup were given. Then each particular cataloging was used to suggest opening phase moves and goals tailored to the given setup.

I argued that some of the opening principles articulated by Aron Nimzovich are more for chess1 than for fundamental chess. Other principles would have been refined or discredited earlier in chess history had chess not been restricted to chess1. These include principles like a knight on the rim is dim, hypermodern centers, and principles judging when it is wise to advance the pawns in front of one's castled king.

The consensus is that an individual game of chess960 morphs into a chess1 game after the first 12 plairs, at the end of the opening phase. I discussed how we should precisely define this merge. I concluded that in one important dimension the merge is complete by the end of the opening, but by other dimensions the merge does not happen until half way through the middle game. Major differences in king fort design were exposed, and these are among the ways chess960 middle games can long remain unmerged with chess1. Using the concept of aggregation, I also explored the idea that perhaps the merge is never total, not even in the endgame phase. The transitive relationship between the opening and endgame is well documented for chess1, and I attempted to extend this same relationship to chess960. It is crucial to understand that an early total merge would be less desirable than the delayed merge I found.

The moves of a chess960 game do not create chaotic or awkward positions. They arise from setups that are as valid as the symmetrical setup of chess1. More to the point, they arise from intelligent logical play, which by definition does not lead to chaotic positions. Players should not mistake variety or unfamiliarity for awkwardness. Chess1 is shown to be incapable of delivering to us all the rich variety that is natural from chess960, and which is all proper for fundamental chess. We have been missing out on a lot of chess beauty, and that is a shame.

Comparing and contrasting play that begins from different setups creates an unlimited variety of statistical comparisons that could raise interesting questions and further our understanding of chess. There is not yet enough data to justify most of the statistical comparisons that will eventually become possible. Yet we did perform a demonstration of the general idea by charting data of castling behavior for different setups.

Trailing Questions to Investigate

White's Advantage: I investigated the consensus idea that White's unfair advantage is even bigger in chess960. By statistical analyses I found this consensus to be unsupported. All the while we know the FFM rule can put this whole unfairness out of chess.

I looked at setups that had the highest and lowest rates of drawn games. The sparse data hint that some setups more easily provide for high quality king forts, and that such king forts occur more frequently in games that end in a draw.

USCF Recognition of Chess960: Finally, I must reiterate my call for the USCF to formally recognize chess960. Above all, the USCF should provide a formal rating into which chess960 results can figure. I recommend allowing chess960 results to apply to the existing ratings. Even if this successfully contributes to many more chess960 tournaments being held, we will find the rating values are unaffected. The reason is that the better chess players will be the better chess960 players also. Chess960 is just chess.

13
Annotated Games

Annotation Format

Chess playing computer programs are imperfect, as are grandmasters. But programs have become tenacious challengers even to grandmasters. So the recommendations of programs are usually respectable or better. In my annotation format, every actual move is accompanied by a specific best move suggestion from a chess program, plus the program's specific numeric evaluation of its best move. Many chess books would instead have whitespace on the remainder of each line, which I do not see as preferable.

There are times when a chess playing program gives out inconsistent or contradictory evaluation values. These are sometimes due to the horizon effect, meaning its total blindness to what might happen after the last ply calculated. There can be other reasons also. Some individual best move suggestions or their evaluations may be inaccurate, as with any human generated annotation. There is no guarantee that the program's suggestions are always among the very best moves.

Overall I feel that together the suggestions and evaluations of the program do much to clarify the trends and crucial points of the game, at a richly granular level. I like the thoroughness of annotating a specific move suggestion for every ply. Each suggestion helps put its corresponding actual move into better perspective. Each suggestion does its part to show the breadth of possible play. We see how easily the game could have veered away in many different directions. I hope this presentation layout makes the program's suggestions and evaluations unobtrusive for people that prefer to ignore them.

Understanding the Program's Suggested Plies: Often the program suggests the same move as the one actually made by the player. This speaks well for both the program and the players. These agreements are represented by an '=' (equals sign), here to be interpreted as "same". It often occurs that the program feels several moves are of roughly equivalent strength. The program may judge its suggested move as no better than the actual move made by the player. The evaluation patterns reveal this well enough.

Understanding the Evaluations: In my presentation, positive values always mean White has the better position, and negatives always favor Black. An evaluation of +.6 means White stands better by slightly more than half a pawn. It is unwise for us to give much weight to minor differences between evaluation values. The player's move may be evaluated at +.3, and the program may prefer its own move at +.4. Differences of +.0 –to– +.3 are usually too slight to be compelling.

In the presentation format below, each evaluation states how the program judges the position as it would have been had the program's move been played. Suppose an annotation shows White actually played 20. Bf2c5, but the program suggested 20. Re2c with an evaluation of +.6. This alone does not tell us how the program evaluated the actual move of Bf2c5. To find the evaluation of the actual move, we need to look at the evaluation given to the move recommended for opponent's next ply. If these two consecutive evaluations are roughly the same, then White's actual Bf2c5 was roughly as good as the suggested Re2c.

Stingy: Programs never give out '!' as annotators, they give out only '?'. This will be more apparent in "rapid" time control games such as these from Mainz. The next step for chess960 should be a grandmaster level tournament with long time controls.

Game 13.1

Levon Aronian – Atanas Kolev, 0-1
Mainz 2005/08, Rd.3, R#913, Game/20 +5 seconds/move

Actual		Computer			
RKNB-QRBN		White		Black	
White	Black	Move	Eval	Move	Eval
Despite this early loss, Kolev was only 1 point behind the leader Aronian after round 8, with 3 rounds remaining. After defeating grandmasters in rounds 7-8, Kolev drew his remaining games. This setup is certainly different from chess1's R#362. Yet overall the attributes of this setup are relatively similar to those of chess1. Its bishops and knights are situated in a manner reminiscent of chess1. Castling short (here 'a' wing) seems preferable.					
1. f24	f75				
2. Nh1g3	e76			Bg8d5	+.1

A classic chess opening pattern, even though the setup
is not R#362. Kolev reacted defensively by choosing
to defend in the model of Philidor, shutting in his Bg8.
The computer prefers to counter-attack with that
bishop, 2... Bg8d5 3. Bg1d4 Qe8f7 4. Qe1f2 Nh8g6
(symmetry), 5. d23 e76 +.1.

| 3. | e24 | f5:e4 | Bg1d4 | +.2 | = | +.2 |
| 4. | Ng3:e4 | Bd8e7 | Bg1d4 | +.2 | Nh8g6 | +.1 |

Computer envisions 4. Bg1d4 Nh8g6 5. Bd4:g7 Rf8:4
6. Rf1:R4 Ng6:Rf4 7. Qe1:4 Qe8f7 +.0.

5.	Nc1d3	Nc8d6	Bd1g4	+.3	Nh8g6	+.4
6.	Ne4c5	Nh8f7	Ne4:Nd6	+.4	Nh8g6	+.2
7.	Bd1f3	c76	=	+.4	=	+.4
8.	a24	Nd6c8	Nd3e5	+.4	g75	+.3

Like some other chess960 games, this one involves
attacking a potential weaknesses on the opponent's
2nd rank (here b7 and d7), using a pattern not identical
to what is usually seen in chess1. Black is losing
tempos in his reactive defensive play, and is falling
behind in development.

In the next plair, if 9... b76 then 10. Ra3b pinning Pb6.

9.	Ra13	Nf7d8	Bg1d4	+.4	Nc8d6	+.4
10.	Ra3b	a75	Nd3e5	+.6	Kb8c7	+.4
11.	Qe14	e65? (D13.1)	Nd3e5	+.4	Kb8c7	+.3
12.	Bf3g4	Be7:Nc5	Bf3g4	+1.9	=	+1.9

The d7 weakness, worsened by 11... e65?, cannot be defended. Aronian looks at the vacated e6 square and pounces. Aronian calculates far ahead to enable him to confidently appear to sacrifice his Rb3 in an exchange. But Aronian will be left with a 2 pawn advantage.

13.	Nd3:Bc5	Bg8:Rb3	=	+2.0	=	+2.1
14.	Nc5:d7#	Kb8c7	=	+2.0	=	+2.1
15.	Nd7:Rf8	Nc8d6	=	+2.1	Bb3:c2	+2.2
16.	Qe4:5	Qe8:Nf	Qe41	+2.2	Bb3:c2	+2.4
17.	c2:Bb3	Ra86	=	+2.8	Nd8f7	+2.7
18.	Qe5d4	Nd8f7	Rf1e	+4.1	=	+2.9
19.	Rf1e	Nf7h6	=	+3.0	=	+3.0
20.	Bg4h3	Nh6f5	Bg4e6	+3.0	Nh6f7	+3.3
21.	Qd4e5	Ra68	=	+3.7	b76	+3.7
22.	g24	Ra8e?	d23	+4.5	b76	+3.9

The computer gives a '?' annotation, but Kolev understood that 23. Qe5:a# would follow. Kolev needs to strive for complication as a last desperate try.

23.	Qe5:a#	Kc7d	=	+7.0	=	+7.0
24.	Re1:R8	Qf8:Re	Re15	+7.2	=	+7.2
25.	g4:Nf5	Qe8h5	=	+7.4	=	+7.4
26.	Qa5c3	0-1	=	+7.4	Qh5d1#	
27.			Kb1a2		Qd1:Bg	

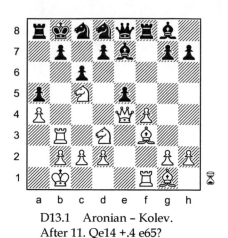

D13.1   Aronian – Kolev.
After 11. Qe14 +.4 e65?
Next 12. Bf3g4 +1.9.

D13.2   Zaitsev - Harikrishna.
After -.1 10. Qe14? c76 -.7
Next 11. Ng3e2 Bh4:Rf2 -1.6.

Game 13.2

Mikhail Zaitsev (IM) – Pente Harikrishna (GM), 0-1
Mainz 2005/08, Rd.3, R#913, Game/20 +5 seconds/move

| | Actual | | Computer | | | |
| | RKNB-QRBN | | White | | Black | |
	White	Black	Move	Eval	Move	Eval
Both players had 2 points at the start of the third round. Both players finished with 7 points, 3 behind winner L.Aronian.						
1.	f24	f75	e24		f6	
2.	Nh1g3	Bg8d5	Bg1d4		e75	
3.	Ng3:f5	Bd5:g2	e24		=	

White's envisioned 3. Ng3:f5 Rf8:N5 4. e24 fork reminds
me of a chess1 Four Knights variation, as in Tarrach -
Lasker Berlin WCC game 3 1916, 1. e24 e76 2. Ng1f3
Nb8c6 3. Nb1c3 Ng8f6 4. Bf1c4 Nf6:e4 5. Nc3:Ne4 d75.

4.	Rf12	Bg2h3	=		Bg2c6	
5.	Nf5g3	e76	Nf5:g7	+.3	=	+.2
6.	Nc1d3	Nc8d6	e24	+.2	d76	.0
7.	e24	Bd8h4	=	+.5	Nd6c4	+.5

It is interesting to see a bishop pinning a knight outside the
confines of chess1. This pin looks exceptionally effective.
The rook and queen are both potential targets. White
is already suffering a lack of space for his vulnerable pieces.

8.	Bd1f3	Nh8g6	Nd3e5	+.6	Nh8f7	+.3
9.	e45?	Nd6f5	Bf3h5	+.4	=	.0

White may have weakened his center by over-advancing
e45. The computer wanted to pin Black's Ng6. After the
first ten plairs, the two armies are nearly fully engaged
in hand-to-hand combat.

10.	Qe14?	c76	Rf2e, or	-.1	=	-.7
		(D13.2)	Bf3g2.			
11.	Ng3e2	Bh4:Rf2	Bf3g2	-.6	=, or	-1.6
					Qe87	

White's chose to suffer an exchange sacrifice rather than
lose a pawn outright by a series of takes on g3. Black
maintains an advantage from here on.

12.	Bg1:Bf2	Nf5h4	=	-1.6	=, or b76	-1.6
13.	Nd3c5	Nh4:Bf3	Bf2c5	-1.5	=	-1.3

If 13. Bf2c5 Bh3f5 14. Qe43 Rf87 Bf3h5 we would see the same pin for White that Black achieved in plair 7.

14.	Qe4:Nf3	Bh3f1	=	-1.3	=	-1.3
15.	Qf3b	b76	=	-1.3	=	-1.3
16.	Ne2d4	Ng6:f4	Ne2g3	-2.8	=	-2.8

White abandons his Pf4 as a lost cause, understandably feeling the need to get more active and aggressive with his pieces. The computer can reassess its earlier evaluations with greater accuracy as the advantages are pressed ever nearer to their more concrete outcomes.

17.	Bf2g3	Nf4e2	a23	-2.8	Kb8c7	-3.1
18.	**Nd4:e6?**	d7:Ne6	Nd4:Ne2	-3.4	=	-4.6

With only limited options, White is fighting and taking risks. But he is mostly hoping for complication and a mistake by his opponent. The 'a' rooks remain conspicuously immobile.

19.	Nc5:e6	Ne2:Bg3	=	-4.6	Rf8g	-4.6
20.	Ne6:Rf8	**Qe8:Nf?**	=	-4.1	Ng3e4	-3.8
21.	Qb3:Ng	Bf1c4	=	-3.1	Bf1e2	-3.1
22.	Kb1c/Rad	Kb87	b23	-2.9	Bc4:a2	-3.0
23.	Qg3h4	Bc4g8	b23	-2.7	=	-2.8
24.	Rd1e	Ra8e	b23	-2.8	h76	-3.2
25.	a24	Qf8e7	Kc1b	-3.1	h76	-3.6

26.	Qh4g3	Re8f	Qh4e	-3.3	Re8d	-3.5
27.	a45	Qf8e7	d24	-3.4	=	-3.6
28.	Qg3d	g76	Re1d	-3.5	Qe7h4	-4.4
29.	Kc1b	Qe7c5	Qd34	-4.1	Rf82	-4.9
30.	a56#	Kb7c	Qd36	-4.6	=	-5.4
31.	b23	Be6f5	Qd3e4	-5.4	Rf8d	-5.8
32.	0-1					

Game 13.3

Ivan Sokolov – Alexey Shirov, 1-0
Mainz 2005/08, Rd.6, R#583, Game/20 +5 seconds/move

Actual		Computer			
RNKN-RBBQ		**White**		**Black**	
White	**Black**	**Move**	**Eval**	**Move**	**Eval**

These two players were among those tied for the lead
half way through the tournament when they met
for this game. This victory helped Sokolov finish in
2nd place, behind only L. Aronian, to whom he
lost in the next round. Shirov finished tied for 4th.

No knight opposition is inherent in this setup. There
will be no rank 2 pawns for king forts on the 'h' wing.
But any 'a' wing forts will be under heavy coordinated
attack along the diagonals, maybe within easy reach
by unopposed enemy 'a' wing knights.

1.	Nb1c3	g76		
2.	f24	Bf8g7		

3.	e24	Nb8c6				
4.	Nd1e3	Nd8e6	Bf1d3	+.2	=	+.1
5.	g23	g65	=	+.2	Kc8/Rad	+.1
6.	Ne3d5	g5:f4	f4:g5	+.6	g5:f4	+.4

Indeed the steeds penetrate early. They have the eye catching potential to exploit the weak rank 2 pawns in column 'c', for a fork of rooks.

7.	g3:f4	Ne6d4	Nd5:f4	+.3	=	+.2
8.	e45	e76?	Nc3a4	+.3	f76	+.1

Plair 8 may be the genesis of Black's loss, even though the evaluation recovered briefly. Black's diagonal pressures from near the h8 corner are stunted from here on.

9.	Nd5b4	f76	=	+.8	a75	+.7
10.	Bg1:Nd4	Nc6:Bd4	Bf1a6	+.7	=	+.4

More aggressive would have been 10. Bf1a6. But Black's Nd4 could not be allowed to stay there for too long, being far more active than White's Bg1.

Next we see White make Black jealous with the excellent activation of his White's Qh1, with tempo. Black misses a crucial opportunity to free his game, and gives White a major advantage. White fails to exploit promptly, so his advantage dissipates.

11.	Qh1e4	Nd4c6? (D13.3)	=	+.3	f6:e5	+.4
12.	Nb4:Nc6	d7:Nc6	=	+2.2	=	+1.9
13.	Kc1/Rad?	Kc8/Rad	Bf1a6	+2.5	f6:e5	+.4

With longer time controls we might have seen 13. Bf1a6
Ra8b 14. Qe4:c6 Re87 15. Nc3b5 giving White scary
pressure on Black's king. But the computer sees no way
to force further material advantage from that variation.

14.	Qe4a	Kc8b	d24	-.2	f6:e5		-.2
15.	Qa4b3	Kb8a	=	.0	=		+.1
16.	Nc3e4	**Rd85?**	=	+.1	f6:e5		+.2

Computer suggests 16... f6:e5 to restrict White to defending
Pe5 with pieces instead of with Pf4. This would deny
White time to play Bf1c4 as an effective threat. For
example, computer calculates 16... f6:e5 17. Ne4c5
Rd8b 18. f4:e5 Re8d 19. d24 h75 20. Bc1f4 Qh86# (+.6).

17.	Bf1c4	Rd54	=	+1.5	Rd58		+1.5
18.	Ne4c5	Re8b	=	+1.6	=		+1.6
19.	Bc4:e6	Bg7f8	=	+1.6	=		+1.6

White is now up 1 pawn in objective material. To the
computer's credit, the evaluations rightly show White's
advantage as even bigger than +1.0, even though no
further material advantage occurs before the game ends.

20.	Ne5d3	Bg8:Be6	c23	+1.8	=		+1.5
21.	Qb3:Be6	f6:e5	=	1.6	=		1.5
22.	f4:e5	**c65?**	=	+1.6	Bf8g7		+1.6

Black now threatens c54 to dislodge White's Nd3 as a
defender of White's passed Pe5. Yet Black now gets
punished for delaying both the clearing of his rank 1, and
the improved coordination of his bishop.

23.	Re1g	Bf8g7	=	+2.7	h75	+2.8
24.	Qe67	c54	=	+2.7	=	+2.5
25.	Rg1:B7	c4:Nd3	=	+2.6	=	+2.6
26.	Qe7:c	d3:c2	c2:d3	+2.5	=	+2.2

White was courageous to let Black play d3:c2, reducing White's endgame material standing, and giving Black a rank 7 passed Pc2. Of course White cannot play 27. Kc1:2?? Rb8c.

27.	Rd1g	Rd48	Rd1f	+2.1	h75	+2.0
28.	e56	Rd8c	=	+2.6	h75	+2.5
29.	Qc7f	Rc8f	=	+2.7	=	+2.7

The next several moves illustrate that there is often no one right move. White's attack had several side streets to choose from.

30.	Qf7c	Rf8c	Qf7h5	+2.8	=	+2.3
31.	Qc7e5	Qh8e	Qc7e	+2.2	h76	+2.3
32.	Rg7d	Rc86	Rg7:h	+2.4	=	+2.4
33.	Rg1e	Rb8c	=	+2.4	h76	+2.4
34.	Qe5b	Rc6b	Qe5d	+3.0	=	+2.4
35.	Qb5d	Qe8h	Qb5f	+2.6	=	+2.6
36.	Qd54	Qh8g	Qd5e	+2.8	=	+2.1
37.	Qd45	Qg8h	Qd4e5	+2.0	=	+2.7
38.	Qd5e	Qh8g	=	+3.2	=	+2.6
39.	Rd7c	Rc8e	b23	+5.5	=	+2.9
40.	Rc7g	1-0	=	+3.3	Qg8h	+3.3

How delightfully odd. Black is the player with the defended rank 7 pawn, yet White's rank 6 passed pawn seems the bigger threat. White has used the greater activity of his pieces in an efficient manner, denying Black the escape tempos he needs.

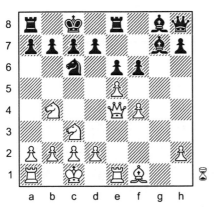

D13.3   Sokolov - Shirov.
After 11. Qh1e4 +.3 Nd4c6?
Next 12. Nb4:Nc6 +2.2.

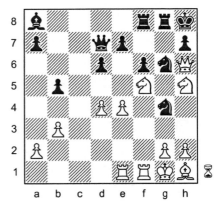

D13.4   Stefanova - Nisipeanu.
After 19. c3:d4 Ne5g4 +.6
Next 20. Qh6d2 e76 +.6

The well known commercial chess program I relied on for suggesting and evaluating every ply sometimes seemed to exaggerate small advantages compared to other engines. In sections of other annotated games I overruled the primary program with the consensus of the others. However, for this next game between Stefanova – Nisipeanu I decided to let the primary program have its say unedited. The program was given seven minutes per move, on a fast computer with lots of memory.

Game 13.4

Antoaneta Stefanova – Liviu-Dieter Nisipeanu, 1-0
Mainz 2005/08, Rd.10, R#472, Game/20 +5 seconds/move

Actual		Computer			
BRNN-QKRB		White		Black	
White	Black	Move	Eval	Move	Eval

Stefanova was competing in the annual chess960 tournament for her second time in two years. Nisipeanu played in 2003 but missed 2004.

	White	Black	Move	Eval	Move	Eval
1.	e24	g76	Kf1g/Rgf	+.2	f75	-.1
2.	Nd1e3	d76	=	+.5	=	+.2
3.	f24	c75	Kf1g/Rgf	+.6	b75	+.6

Clearly the computer's absolute evaluation values are inflated. Their relative values may often be reasonable. The computer's suggested moves may still be strong.

	White	Black	Move	Eval	Move	Eval
4.	b23	Bh8:Ba1	=	+.8	=	+.8
5.	Rb1:Ba	b75	=	+.8	=	+.8
6.	d23	Kf8g/Rgf	Qe1h4	+.8	Kf8g/Rgf	+.4

An interesting pawn formation rarely seen within the confines of chess1. What can Black do with his 'a' wing space advantage? Does either king have a safe future? Black seems underdeveloped heading into plair 7, but the two players are equally developed.

White's next ten plies all move force toward the 'h' wing for a possible attack on Black's king.

7.	f45	Nc8b6	=	+.6	g6:f5	+.6
8.	Qe1h4	Nd8c6	Kf1g/Rgf	+.9	=	+.8
9.	Kf1g/Rgf	Nc6e5	Nc1e2	+.8	=	+.8
10.	Nc1e2	Nb6d7	c23	+.9	Nb8d7	+.8
11.	Ne2f4	Kg8h	Ra1d	+.8	Kg8h	+.8
12.	Qh46	Rf8g	Ra1d	+.8	=	+.4
13.	f5:g6	Ne5:g6	=	+.4	=	+.4
14.	Ne3f5	Nd7e5	a23	+.4	=	+.4
15.	Nf4h5	f76	Qh63	+.4	=	+.1
16.	Ra1e	Qe8d7	Qh6e3	+.1	=	+.1

White has threatened Black's king, but now her attack begins to weaken.

17.	c23	Rb8f	=	+.1	b54	+.1
18.	d34	c5:d4	Qh6d2	+.6	=	+.6
19.	c3:d4	Ne5g4 (D13.4)	=	+.6	Ne5f7	+.6
20.	Qh6d2	e76	=	+.6	=	+.6
21.	Nf5g3	f65	Nf5e3	+.5	=	+.4
22.	e4:f5	e6:f5	=	+.4	=	+.4
23.	h23	Ng4f6	=	+.4	=	+.4
24.	Nh5:Nf6	Rf8:N6	=	+.4	=	+.4
25.	d45	Ng6e5	Ng3h5	+.4	=	+.4
26.	Ng3h5	Rf6g	=	+.4	Rf68	+.3

Black now looks to have the potential to turn the tables and become the attacker. If it were Black's turn to move, he might consider Qd7f. The White Nh5 is unprotected, and this move pressures White's crucial Pd5, which blocks Black's Ba8.

243

27.	Qd24	h76?	g23	+.5	Rg8e	+.5

Play might have gone 27... Rg8e 28. Re13 Rg65 29. Nh5f4 Qd7g 30. Rf1d Kh8g 31. a23 h76 with positions held.

28.	Re1:N5	1-0	=	+2.7	d6:Re5
29.			Qd4:e5#		Kh87
30.			Rf1:5		Rg8e
31.			Nh5f6#		Rg6:Nf
32.			Qe5:Rf6		Qd7g

##

244

Diagram Classification
Answers

Chapter 8

mga_1* from live games:

mga_11: P.Svidler – M.Kazhgaleyev, 2002/08, R#795 - S#832, BBRK-NRQN.

mga_12: A.Kosteniuk – I.Sokolov, 2005/08, R#913 - S#829, RKNB-QRBN, after 24. Rf1:Rd.

mgi_2* chess960 games:

mgi_20: A.Huzman – F.Vallejo Pons, 2003/08, R#155 - S#393, QRNB-BNKR, after 12... Bd8b6.

mgi_23: M.Schulz – E.Bacrot, 2004/08, R#041 - S#876, QBRK-RNBN, after 12. ... Ng6e7.

mgi_2* chess1 games:

mgi_21: I.Sokolov – E.Agrest, 2003/08, chess1, after 12... Bb4d6.

mgi_22: R.Kazimdzhanov – A.Huzman, 2003/08, chess1, after 12... e6:d5.

mgb_3* chess960 games:

mgb_30: L.McShane - V.Zvaginsev, 2004/08, R#112 - S#001, BBQN-NRKR, after 19. Nd4b5.

mgb_31: V.Zvaginsev – A.Shchekachev, 2004/08, R#406 - S#142, NRQN-KBBR, after 16. b24.

mgb_36: D.Sadvakasov – F.Levin, 2004/08, R#315 - S#409, RQNB-BNKR, after 18... Qb8f4.

mgb_37: A.Shirov - L.Aronian, 2005/08, R#472 - S#435, BRNN-QKRB, after 18. c4:Nd5.

mgb_3* chess1 games:

mgb_32: I.Farago – E.Bacrot, 2004/08, chess1, after 17... Re8:R3.

mgb_33: A.Berelovich – A.Graf, 2004/08, chess1, after 17. Qd41.

mgb_34: R.Vaganian – V.Zvaginsev, 2004/08, chess1, after 17... Nd5f6.

mgb_35: E.Bacrot – A.Eisenbeiser, 2004/08, chess1, after 17... Ra85.

mgf_4* chess960 games:

mgf_41: M.Kobalija – K.Sasihiran, 2004/08, R#406 - S#142, NRQN-KBBR, after 24. d45.

mgf_43: A.Stefanova - A.Yusupov, 2005/08, R#181 - S#794, RQKN-BBRN, after 22... Nc6b4.

mgf_44: A.Yusupov – L.Aronian, 2005/08, R#130 - S#096, BBQN-RNKR, after 25. Qd13.

mgf_4* chess1 games:

mgf_40: I.Sokolov – W.Uhlmann, 2005/08, chess1, after 24. d56.

mgf_42: I.Khenkin – A.Morozevich, 2005/08, chess1, after 24... Ba3:c5.

mgf_45: A.Dreev – T.Hermann, 2005/08, chess1, after 33. Bc1d2.

Chapter 9

egk_5* from live games:

egk_50: R.Ruck – R.Vaganian, 2005/08, R#472 - S#435, BRNN-QKRB, after 111... Kg6f5.

egk_53: E.Lobron – A.Shirov, 2005/08, R#785 - S#941, RKRB-NQBN, after 57... Ka43.

egk_5* derived from puzzles:

egk_51: Derived from The Complete Studies of Genrikh Kasparyan, edited by A. John Roycroft. #027.

egk_52: Again, dervived from Kasparyan, #028.

egy_6* chess960 games:

egy_60: A.Morozevich – N.Khurtsidze, 2005/08, R# - S#145, BNRB-NQKR, after 63... Nc5b7.

egy_6* chess1 games:

egy_61: D.Fridman – A.Aleksandrov, 2003/08, chess1, after 56. Be6d7.

Bibliography

Print Publications

Chess (the British magazine): 2004/05, page 51.

Chess Life magazine; USCF.

Evans, Larry: *The 10 Most Common Chess Mistakes...and How to Avoid Them!*; Cardoza 1998. ISBN 1-58042-042-7.

Fine, Reuben: *Chess the Easy Way*; Cornerstone 1941.

Gligoric, Svetozar: *Shall We Play Fischerandom Chess?*; Batsford 2002. ISBN 0-7134-8764-X.

Hopper, Millard: *Win at Checkers*; Dover 1941. ISBN 0-486-20363-8.

Hort, Vlastimil: *The Modern Defense*; R.H.M. Press 1979. ISBN 0-89058-040-5.

King, Daniel & Pietro Ponzetto: *Mastering the Spanish*; Henry Holt 1993. ISBN 0-8050-3278-9.

Kmoch, Hans: *Pawn Power in Chess*; Dover 1990 (repro of 1959). ISBN 0-486-26486-6.

Lane, Gary: *How to Attack in Chess*; Batsford ICE 1996. ISBN 1-879479-39-7.

Maxwell, Jonathan: *Blitz Theory*; Silent Lyric Productions 2005. ISBN 0967775205.

Mednis, Edmar: *From the Opening Into the Endgame*; Everyman (or Cadogan) 1983. ISBN 1-85744-124-9.

Nimzovich, Aron (edited by Fred Reinfeld): *My System*; David McKay Co. 1947 (originally 1929). ISBN 0-769-14025-5.

Nunn, John: *Secrets of Grandmaster Chess*; ICE-Batsford 1997. ISBN 1-879479-54-0.

Nunn, John: *Solving in Style*; Gambit 2002. ISBN 1-901983-66-8.

Nunn, John: *Understanding Chess Move by Move*; Gambit 2001. ISBN 1-901983-41-2.

Pandolfini, Bruce: *Weapons of Chess*; Simon & Schuster 1989. ISBN 0-671-65972-3.

Peters, Jack: the column *Chess* in the *Los Angeles Times*; 2004.

Philidor, Andre: Analysis of the Game of Chess; 1749, 1817 republication.

Polgar, Laszlo: *Chess: 5334 Problems, Combinations, and Games*; Black Dog & Leventhal 1995. ISBN 1-884822-31-2.

Roycroft, John A. (Ed.): *The Complete Studies of Genrikh Kasparyan*; Russell Enterprises 1997. ISBN 1-888690-02-X.

Scharnagl, Reinhard: *Fischer-Random-Chess (FRC/Chess960): The Revolutionary Future of Chess (Including Computer Chess)*; BoD GmbH, Norderstedt 2004. ISBN 3-8334-1322-0.

Shirov, Alexei: *Fire on the Board*; Cadogan, 1997. ISBN 1-85744-150-8.

Silman, Jeremy: *How to Reassess Your Chess* (3rd ed.); Siles Press 1997. ISBN 1-890085-00-6.

Speelman, Jon: *Jon Speelman's Best Games*; International Chess Ent. 1997. ISBN 1-879479-60-5.

Watson, John: *Secrets of Modern Chess Strategy: Advances Since Nimzowitsch*; Gambit 1998. ISBN 1-901983h-07-2

Morris, William (Ed.): *The American Heritage Dictionary*; Houghton Mifflin, 1969. LCCN 76-86995.

Yrjola, Jouni & Jussi Tella: *An Explosive Chess Opening Repertoire for Black*; Gambit 2001. ISBN 1-901983-50-1.

Http:// Web Sites

AaronTay.per.sg/Winboard/

Chess-960.com

ChessAntique.com (Jon Crumiller)

ChessBox.de , Smirf.de (Reinhard Scharnagl)

ChessCafe.com

ChessTigers.de (or .org)

ChessGames.com

ChessVariants.com

en.Wikipedia.org/wiki/Chess960/

EnPassant.dk (diagram font Chess Alpha by Eric Bentzen, permission)

GeoCities.com/SiliconValley/Lab/73 78/ (Bill Wall)

Wikipedia.org/wiki/chess960

HouseOfStaunton.com

JimLoy.com , UsaCheckers.com

NWChess.com

PlayWithArena.com

ShredderChess.com

SilentLyricProductions.com

UsChess.org (USCF)

Chessville.com

ChessBase.com

www.evonet.be/~marcsmet/ebbs/ download/FRC_960Pos.pdf (F.Joseph)

hano53433838.web.infoseek.co.jp/li st/p_50/50_0.htm (*Chess* 2004/05)

Your feedback is welcomed.

We are always interested to receive feedback on this book, or on any other book from Castle Long Publications. Please let us know if you have suggestions for enhancing a possible revised edition. Or let us know what aspects of the work are relatively strong or weak (including ideas, theories, proofreading oversights, diagram errors etc).

At CLP we would be happy to help publicize chess960 news and events occurring anywhere on the planet. Feel free to ask us to link to your chess960 topics, or for us to post news about an upcoming or recently completed chess960 event.

Please see our web site **http://CastleLong.com/** for contact and other information, and for items of general chess interest.

(mh75c)

Printed in the United States
72570LV00003B/75